Spectacular
scraps

A SIMPLE APPROACH TO STUNNING QUILTS

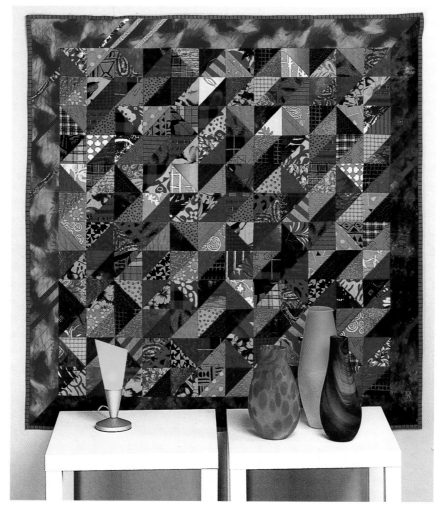

*Judy*Hooworth *Margaret*Rolfe

SALLY MILNER PUBLISHING

EDITORIAL
MANAGING EDITOR
Judy Poulos
EDITORIAL ASSISTANT
Ella Martin
JUNIOR PRODUCTION EDITOR
Heather Straton

PHOTOGRAPHY
Andy Payne, Richard Weinstein
STYLING
Kathy Tripp

PRODUCTION AND DESIGN
PRODUCTION DIRECTOR
Anna Maguire
PRODUCTION COORDINATOR
Meredith Johnston
DESIGN MANAGER
Drew Buckmaster
ASSISTANT DESIGNER
Sheridan Packer

PUBLISHED BY Sally Milner Publishing Pty Ltd
734 Woodville Road
BINDA NSW 2583
AUSTRALIA
www.sallymilner.com.au

PRINTED BY Toppan Printing Co. Hong Kong
REPRINTED 1999, 2000, 2001, 2003, 2004, 2006
© Judy Hooworth and Margaret Rolfe

SPECTACULAR SCRAPS
ISBN-13 978 1 86351 272 5
ISBN-10 1 86351 272 1

Contents

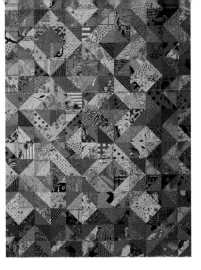

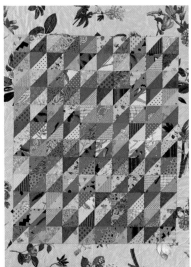

The authors

Judy Hooworth is a leading Australian quiltmaker. Originally trained in art and illustration through studies at the National Art School in Sydney, Judy first became an art teacher. In the 1970s she saw quilts in glossy American magazines and began making quilts herself, primarily learning by doing. Other women in the North Sydney area were also interested in quilts, and they began meeting weekly. Later Judy joined with Noreen Dunn to make quilts on commission. Throughout all this, she was always interested in contemporary quilts and made her own original work. Judy has exhibited in the annual exhibitions of the New South Wales Quilters' Guild and has been involved in most of Australia's contemporary quilt exhibitions. She was a key organizer of the New Quilt exhibitions of contemporary quilts held at the Manly Art Gallery and Museum. In 1995, Judy received a grant from the Visual Arts/Crafts Fund from the Australia Council. In 1992, one of Judy's quilts was selected for Visions – The Art of the Quilt, San Diego. Judy has also successfully entered quilts in Quilt National, with "Composition in Yellow" selected in 1993 and "Mothers/Daughters #6: Lines of Communication" selected in 1999. Judy has taught quiltmaking throughout Australia, in New Zealand and Germany, and continues to make her own art quilts.

Margaret Rolfe is a well-known Australian quiltmaker, author and quilt historian. She was inspired to take up quiltmaking because of quilts she saw in America in 1975, the year before the American Bicentennial. Returning to Australia, Margaret helped found the group that has now become Canberra Quilters. In the early 1980s, Margaret created pieced and appliqué designs for Australian flowers, animals and birds, and these were published in *Australian Patchwork* in 1985. Her research into the history of quilts led to the book *Patchwork Quilts in Australia* in 1987. Margaret has continued to make quilts and write books about quiltmaking, with a special focus on designing pieced animal and bird blocks. Some of her recent books, published by That Patchwork Place, are *Go Wild with Quilts* (1993) and *Go Wild with Quilts – Again* (1995), which give patchwork designs for North American wildlife, and *A Quilter's Ark* (1997), a selection of animal designs for foundation piecing.

Margaret's most recent book, *Australian Quilt Heritage*, published by J.B. Fairfax Press, is her second book about the history of Australian quilts, from convict-made quilts to the present quilt revival.

Acknowledgments

We specially thank Kerry Gavin, Beryl Hodges, Helen Gray, Carol Richards and Donna Ward for generously lending their wonderful quilts for photography.

The authors are grateful to Dianne Neumann and her staff at The Patchwork Shop, Gold Creek Village, Canberra, for the excellence of their custom machine-quilting.

Our heartfelt thanks to our husbands and families for all their help and support while we worked on this book.

Introduction

This book had its beginning in a workshop called "Scrapaholics Heaven", devised by Judy. The workshop itself was partly inspired by a book called *Half Square Triangles: Exploring Design*, by Barbarah Johannah, which revealed the possibilities of the half-square triangle. But color and fabric are Judy's preoccupation, so the workshop she created centered on color and fabric, as well as on designs created from half-square triangles. Her concept was simple – two colors applied to a Four-patch block made up entirely of half-square triangles.

Margaret attended one of Judy's workshops and was immediately entranced with the possibilities of color and design from this seemingly simple starting point. Believing Judy had something new to add to the literature on scrap quilts, Margaret persuaded Judy that a book was more than just a good idea and should become a reality. Eventually it was decided that the book would be done as a joint project with Judy contributing the original concept and quilts with her magnificent sense of color, and Margaret contributing her writing skills and a second pair of hands to explore the multitude of possibilities.

This book works at many levels. Fundamentally, it will give you a simple way to design and make scrap quilts. The sewing skills involved are all very easy and the quilts are finished with straightforward quilting, which can be done either by machine or by hand. But beyond this, it will offer paths for the exploration of the three fundamentals of quiltmaking: color, fabric and design.

Color is always the most striking feature of quilts, yet it is usually the area about which quilters are least confident. Working on the formula for making scrap quilts, given in this book, you inevitably will be led on a journey of learning about color. The more you experiment and put different fabrics together, the more you will learn and gain confidence. And all the while, you will be making wonderful quilts.

These scrap quilts are a delight for the fabric lover and the dedicated fabric collector – which most quilters are. It was not for nothing that Judy's original workshop was called Scrapaholic's Heaven! All the fabrics you have collected can be used in a rich and satisfying way. More is more in our approach to scrap quilts. Your fabric collection is your resource, and now there is a purpose for absolutely every one of those fabrics – the funny little bits and the long lengths, the pretty ones and the ugly ones, the pieces that did not fit in and the leftovers of the ones that did, the fabrics you have inherited, the ones bought at sales, the pieces swapped or given as gifts, the bright prints, the dull prints, spots, stripes, plaids, florals – in fact, fabrics of every hue and every possible printed design. All those pieces that were so irresistible at the time – now there is a place for them all. This book will help you make inroads into that stash, because the quilts of *Spectacular Scraps* are stash busters!

The design possibilities are endless in what is apparently a very simple Four-patch block. Take four squares, each made up of two half-square triangles in two different colors and there are no less than 256 ways of putting those squares together! See for yourself on page 11. Combine these possibilities with the usual ways of making patterns from units – repetition, reversal and rotation – and the possibilities become truly awesome.

The approach to making our scrap quilts is essentially very straightforward, yet it is also capable of infinite variation. We promise you a lot fun and a lot of great quilts. And we also promise that no two quilts will ever look alike!

Materials and equipment

FABRICS

A wide selection of cotton fabrics is needed for these quilts. Fabrics manufactured especially for quilters are suitable, but cotton dressmaking and decorator fabrics of a similar weight to quilting fabrics can also be used. Some decorator fabrics that are a little heavier can be incorporated, especially if you are machine-piecing and machine-quilting. Look for repeating designs that can make wonderful borders, and also for bold, large prints. While we generally use prints, plain fabrics (solids) can also be used to add splashes of pure color.

We suggest you pre-wash and press all fabrics before use, to ensure that there will be no color bleeding or shrinkage later.

BATTING

Either cotton or polyester batting, or a blend of both, is suitable.

THREADS

For piecing, use a thread suitable for machine-sewing. For most quilts, choose either a neutral-coloured thread, such as grey, or choose a thread to match one of your chosen colours. White or beige thread can be used for light-coloured quilts and black thread for dark-coloured quilts. For machine-quilting, choose a machine-sewing thread in a suitable colour to blend with the patchwork or else use a clear monofilament thread. Cotton quilting thread is required for hand-quilting.

SEWING MACHINE

A machine is your main tool (unless you choose to hand-piece). A $1/4$" (7.5 mm) foot is useful for piecing and a walking foot for machine-quilting. Maintain your machine as suggested by the manufacturer, oiling it regularly and replacing blunt needles immediately.

PINS AND NEEDLES

Accurate cutting and sewing will ensure that these quilts are put together with hardly any pinning. However, pins are useful at times, especially at seam junctions and for use as markers. A hand-sewing needle is required to stitch binding down. Quilting needles, called betweens, are needed if the quilt is to be hand-quilted.

SCISSORS

Keep a small, sharp pair of scissors handy for snipping threads. A pair of dressmaking scissors is needed if you choose not to use a rotary cutter for cutting out the fabrics.

ROTARY CUTTING EQUIPMENT

The quickest and easiest way to make these quilts is to use rotary cutting techniques, and for this you require a rotary cutter, self-healing cutting mat and clear acrylic rulers. A rotary cutter with a blade that is $1^3/4$" (4.5 cm) in diameter is ideal. Replace the blade as soon as it does not cut cleanly. The mat should be at least 12" × 18" (30 cm × 45 cm). A larger mat enables you to make longer cuts. Rulers should be clearly marked with $1/8$" (5 mm) intervals. It is best to have two rulers: a 6" × 24" (15 cm × 60 cm) ruler for long cuts and a 6" × 12" (15 cm × 30 cm) ruler for short cuts. A 6" (15 cm) square ruler is useful for making half-square triangle units from bias strips and also for trimming pieced squares.

PRESSING EQUIPMENT

An iron is essential. Also have a spray bottle full of water for pressing stubborn bits, and a pressure can of spray starch.

MEASUREMENTS

Measurements in this book are given in both the imperial system (inches) and metric system (centimeters and millimeters). Note that they are NOT exact equivalents, but rather equivalents that work in practice using whole numbers or convenient parts of numbers. So 2" becomes 5 cm, 3" becomes 8 cm, 4" becomes 10 cm, and so on. The measurements are not interchangeable, and only one system should be used throughout a project. For seam allowances, the $1/4$" seam allowance is used in the imperial system, and 7.5 mm (0.75 cm) seam allowance in the metric system.

The *Spectacular Scraps* approach

While there are many ways of making scrap quilts, this book describes a particular approach that uses two color families. Fabrics from these two colors are used to create a simple Four-patch block made up of four squares each comprising two half-square triangles.

COLOR AND FABRIC CHOICE

Choose a wide range of hues.

Choosing fabrics is what scrap quilts are all about. Our approach is to make these fabric choices from two color families. We stress the word 'family' here because you need to put together as wide a selection of fabrics as possible of each of your two chosen colors.

There are three major dimensions to choosing the fabrics in your chosen color – color hue, tonal value and printed design.

Firstly, there is the dimension of the color itself. Choose fabrics from a wide dimension of hues within your color. For example, if you choose red, choose all kinds of reds, from orange/reds through to blue/reds and purple/reds.

It is also possible to choose fabrics that are close relatives to your color, so if you choose red as one of your color families, you may also include purples and oranges, as these colors are near red in the color spectrum (in paint, both orange and purple are formed by mixing red with other colors – red with yellow for orange, red with blue for purple).

Secondly, there is the dimension of value how light or dark the color is. Choose

Add related colours.

Vary the tonal value.

from a wide variety of values for your color. In the red family, you would include rose pinks through to maroons and browns. Always include plenty of mid-tone values.

Thirdly, there is the dimension of the printed pattern on the fabrics. Again, look for a wide selection of prints – florals, checks, stripes, both small and large prints, interesting hand-dyed fabrics, multicolored and monochromatic prints. As we are talking families, it is important to remember that all families have their funny members. So this is your chance to include your funnies – the odd fabrics, the uglies, the strange ones.

The reason for this approach is that these variations of

Include a variety of prints.

color, tonal value and printed pattern create interest in the quilt. The underlying pattern is kept constant – the two colors will *always* be put in the same place in the design – but changes are introduced through the variations in the range of colors, the range of tonal values and the variety of prints. The quilt will be more interesting because the pattern will not be a constant repetition of dark and light, the same colors and similar prints. If the darks and lights are kept the same, the colors the same, and the prints the same, the result can be a boring quilt because it is all predictable. The eye can take in the pattern in one glance and has no interest in looking further. But with the two-color family approach, which gives variation in color, tonal value and prints, you will find that elements of the pattern will advance and recede, creating the feeling of multi-layered space. The eye will not be bored, but will rove around, taking in both the underlying pattern and the variations that occur. The quilt will get the ultimate accolade – the second and third look.

We stress this issue of space because, in the final analysis, space is what it is all about. If you have only two different fabrics (one of each color), what you see is one making background and one making foreground. But if within each of these colors there is variation of color, of tonal value, and of prints, then both the background and the foreground will appear to have many layers, as if parts of the design are at many different distances either nearer or farther away.

KEEPING THE COLOR PLACEMENT CONSISTENT

It is essential in this approach that the underlying arrangement of the two colors always remains the same. Once you have chosen the block design and which color family goes in which part of the design, then it is important to adhere to this formula. For example, if your two color families are blue and yellow, always keep the blues and yellows in the same positions in the design, regardless of tonal values (the lights and darks). As one color usually will be the darker of the two, the pattern generally will be carried by the differences between the darks and lights. But if you follow our principles of choosing a wide range of fabrics, sometimes there will be a lighter one where there is usually a darker one. For example, in a blue-and-yellow combination, generally the yellow will be the lighter color and the blue will be the darker color. But a dark mustard yellow may be paired with a light blue, so the light/dark relationship will be reversed. It is important to leave the colors in their place. These reversals will enhance your quilt by making it more interesting because it is not entirely predictable.

Some fabrics will combine both color families. It is easy to assign them to one family or the other if one color predominates. However, if both colors are nearly equal, it may not be so easy to allocate them to one or the other. These crossover fabrics are important to use, as they introduce another point of interest in the quilt because they can soften the lines in the design. So you decide which color family they should join, and keep placing them in the position of this color.

VARIATIONS

Within this approach to scrap quilts, it is possible to make many variations. To begin with, while we always stress having two color families, you can define the families in either a narrow or broad way, rather like the immediate family and the extended family. For example, if blue is your color family, you can use the entire extended family of blues by including blue-related colors, such as purple and turquoise. Or you may stick to only the immediate blue family, although you should still use as many blues as possible, such as violet/blues, green/blues and grey/blues.

To achieve a contemporary look, choose bold colors and large vibrant prints. Big prints and splashy prints often include many other colors besides your chosen color. In fact, it is possible that none of your chosen color appears in some of the triangles after they have been cut out. Don't worry – just keep putting the fabric in its place in the design. The 'surprise' will add interest to the quilt.

Another variation is to limit the tonal range. For example, if you want to make a pretty pastel quilt, you may limit your tonal values to a range between light and middle tones. But even so the same principles will apply – a range of hues within the color, a variation within the chosen tonal range, and a variety of prints in terms of scale and pattern. (See "Lavender's Green", page 46.) Alternatively, you can decide to limit the tonal values from the middle of the range to the darks for a deep, rich effect. Again, within this range, there should be as wide a variation as possible. (See "Black Opal", page 42).

A further variation is to follow the formula with two tonal ranges, such as one going from dark to light and another going from only mid-tone to dark. This creates two areas of shading in the quilt. For example, "Tiger Eyes" on page 74 has the area of light to dark range in the center of the quilt, and the mid-tone to dark range around it.

Another variation is to group the fabrics around a theme or a theme fabric. For example, a teddy bear fabric in blue and caramel inspired the baby quilt on page 50, so blue and caramel became the two color families of the quilt. Likewise, in the quilt "Gathering Rosebuds" on page 36, the theme was floral fabrics in pink and blue. A great border fabric can also be a starting point, such as the blue and yellow print in "Bonjour Paris" on page 38.

Using a color and white is yet another variation. This is different from the two-color approach in that white and a color create a monochromatic color scheme. It is less possible to have fabrics that swap positions through their tonal variation. However, our approach of varying the tonal range, the kind of print and the range of colors still applies. For a monochromatic example, see "Etoile" on page 62.

LIMITATIONS

Are there limitations to the *Spectacular Scraps* approach? We have found that while any two colors can be used to make successful quilts, if there is too great a difference between the tonal values between the two colors, the result may be less than successful. For example, if purple and yellow are the chosen colors, it may not work so well if predominantly pale and pastel yellows are combined with dark purples. However, if the yellow is a stronger color, including the deep yellows, mustards and oranges, there is no reason why a combination such as purple and yellow could not work very well indeed.

If you have a lot of fabrics with small prints and monochromatic colors, it may be best to choose a smaller triangle for your quilt, as the color may look rather flat in larger triangles without the interest of big prints.

HOW MUCH FABRIC DO YOU NEED?

It is impossible to give precise quantities for scrap quilts because, by definition, they are meant to be made from all sorts and sizes of fabric. For the projects in this book, we give you an estimate of the total amount of fabric required so that you will have some idea of the yardage (meterage) required. We cannot be more precise than this and still keep to the principles of our approach to making scrap quilts.

More is better when it comes to these scrap quilts. Of course, smaller quilts will require fewer fabrics, so that a quilt made of sixty-four half-square triangle units will not need as many as one made of 144 or 400 half-square triangle units.

However, some quick rules of thumb may be applied, working from the number of half-square triangle units in the quilt. First, estimate how many of these units will be required for your quilt. For the projects in this book, that number is given in the first step of "Construction". Basing your estimate on four half-square triangles of each fabric (which means cutting two squares from each fabric, if you are cutting triangles from squares), divide the number of half-square triangle units by four. For example, for sixty-four half-square triangle units, the answer is sixteen, so you will need approximately sixteen fabrics from each color family. For a large quilt, you might like to base your estimate on cutting eight half-square triangles from each fabric (which means cutting four squares from each fabric), so you would divide the number of half-square triangle units by eight instead of four. For example, for 400 half-square triangle units, you would need fifty fabrics from each color family.

Alternatively, if you want to work from the number of fabrics you have already acquired, divide the number of fabrics into the number of half-square triangle units. For example, if the number of half-square triangle units is 144 and you have thirty-six fabrics from each color family, divide 144 by thirty-six making four. Therefore you will need to cut four half-square triangles from each of your fabrics. Divide this number by two to determine how many squares to cut for the required number of triangles.

In real life, you are more likely to have twenty-nine fabrics, or some other odd number. The same process as described above will give you an approximation of how many squares to cut from each fabric. For example, 144 divided by 29 is 4.96, so you need to cut about five triangles from each fabric. If you are cutting triangles from squares, it would be easiest to cut two squares from each fabric, then cut another square from half the fabrics. Use a calculator for these odd numbers.

Note that some fabrics can count as more than one because they have different areas of pattern that can be cut up to look like different fabrics.

Quilt design

All the quilts are made using just one shape – a half-square triangle. This triangle is the shape that is created when a square is divided across the diagonal into two equal halves. By definition, it is a right-angle triangle.

The quilt designs in this book are created from a square unit made up of two half-square triangles. In each unit, one triangle is taken from one of the chosen color families and the other triangle is taken from the second color family. This remains constant throughout the quilt; every square is made up of two triangles, one each from the two color families.

When two different colors are used in this way, note that there are four different positions possible for this square unit.

When four of these units are put together, they become what is called a Four-patch block – a patchwork block divisible by four.

As we have already noted, within this seemingly simple block there are no less than 256 ways that the eight triangles can be arranged to make different Four-patch blocks. This is because $4 \times 4 \times 4 \times 4 = 256$. All these possibilities are illustrated below. The concept of all these possibilities is not new. It was first worked out by the French monk, Dominique Douat, and was published in a paper in 1704.

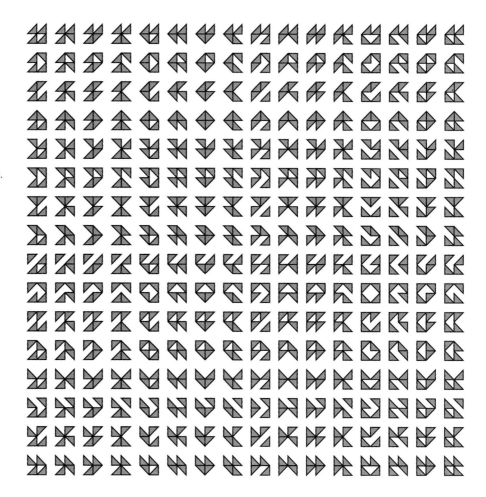

To create quilt designs using these blocks of half-square triangles, the blocks must be repeated in some way. There are three ways of making a pattern with multiples of the same block or same unit of design:

1   Repeat the block

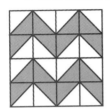

Besides these three possibilities, there is always the option of reversing the colors to create a different effect. You will find that reversing the color changes some designs more than others, depending on the positive and negative spaces created.

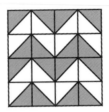 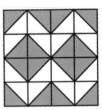 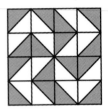

2   Rotate the block around an axis (which means the block is turned 90° from one of its corners)

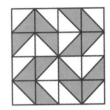

Other design possibilities include:

4   Combining two different blocks

  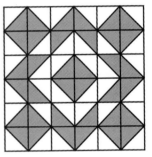

3   Reverse the block

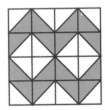

5   Reversing or rotating two or more blocks together

 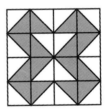

In practice, not all the possible combinations may be useful for quiltmaking – although we don't claim to have explored absolutely all of them! From experience, we have found the following fifteen blocks to be the most interesting. We present these fifteen with some ideas of how the blocks can be arranged to create great quilt designs.

Note how exciting secondary designs can develop when the blocks are repeated in different ways.

■ **Block 1** This block looks like a chevron and it forms strong zigzag designs. See this block used in "Redcurrent" (page 54), "Bonjour Paris" (page 38), "Star Trek" (page 69) and "Hot August Night" (page 64). It is reversed in "Dit, Dot, Dash – Ginger Meggs' Mother Wears Spots" (page 70) and rotated in "Swizzle" (page 30).

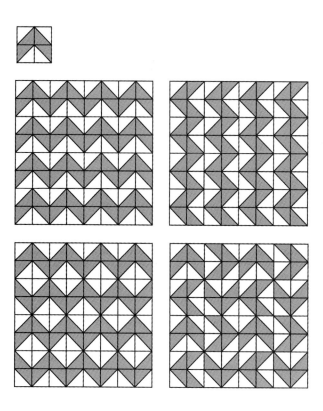

■ **Block 2** The triangle units form a diamond in this design. See this block used in "Find the Froggies" (page 56) and as one of the blocks in "Bonjour Paris" (page 38). When two of these blocks are combined with the colors alternating in their centers (they are positive and negative versions of the block), they make a wonderful pattern that crisscrosses the quilt. Note that this pattern needs an uneven number of blocks to fully develop. See this combination in "Earthworks" (page 67) and "Yellow and Blue" (page 63).

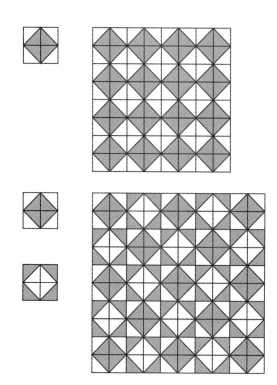

■ **Block 3** While this block appears to be very different from Block 2, when rotated it forms the same pattern as the positive/negative combination of Block 2 given on page 13. However, note that the pattern begins in a different place, so it has a different look. See this block in "Summer Peaches" (page 48).

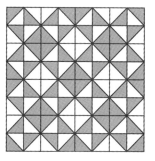

■ **Block 4** The block creates a stripe that can then be repeated or rotated to make many different patterns. See this block in "Gathering Rosebuds" (page 36), "Summer" (page 34), "Teddy Bears' Picnic" (page 50),"Cross of Amethyst" (page 61) and "Masquerade" (page 66).

■ **Block 6** This block is similar to the previous block, but the "tail" is given a twist. Note that this "tail" can be twisted either way. The block creates a strong diagonal pattern when repeated. See this block in "Octopus' Garden" (page 40) and "Singing in the Rain" (page 72).

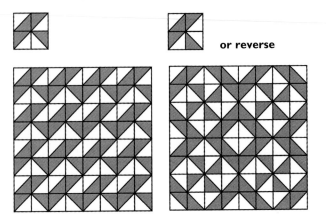

or reverse

■ **Block 7** The triangles form two parallelograms. Note that this block also has a reverse version. See this block in "Kandy Kisses" (page 58) and rotated in "Noel" (page 32).

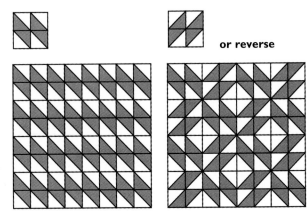

or reverse

■ **Block 5** The block design looks like a bird, but it creates wonderful diamonds when it is rotated. See this block in "Singing the Blues" (page 52), "Sunset Over the Sea" (page 65), "Always Look on the Bright Side" (page 68), "Red Earth, Blue Sky – My Australia" (page 71) and "Tiger Eyes" (page 74).

 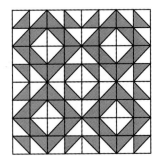

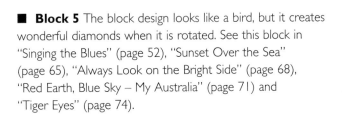

■ Block 8 The triangles form the traditional Flying Geese pattern. See this block in "Lavender's Green" (page 46). When rotated, the traditional Dutchman's Puzzle block is formed.

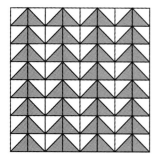
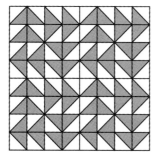

■ Block 9 This is the traditional quilt design known as the Pinwheel. See this block in "Printemps" (page 73).

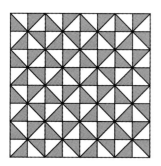

■ Block 10 The triangles form a shape like a goose's head, and when reversed, make the traditional block called Brown Goose. See this block in "Rainforest Rhythms" (page 44).

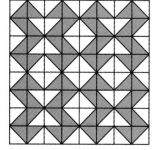
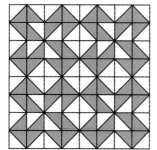

■ Block 11 The triangles form a pyramid design. See this block in "Twilight Roses" (page 60).

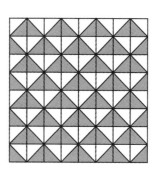

■ Block 12 The straight repetition of the triangle units makes scintillating patterns when rotated and repeated. See this block in "Black Opal" (page 42).

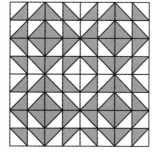
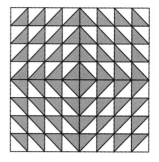

■ Block 13 While the block design looks like an envelope, a star pattern emerges when the blocks are rotated. See this block in "Etoile" (page 62).

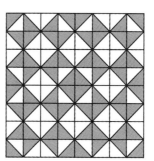

■ **Block 14** The two triangles of this block make the traditional pattern Broken Dishes.

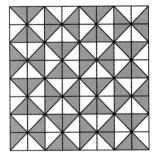 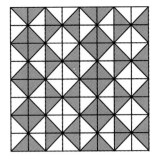

■ **Block 15** An eight-pointed star forms when this block is repeated.

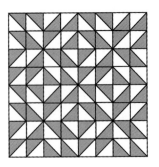

Besides the block designs, it is also possible to use the half-square triangle units to make further designs within a quilt, such as creating a border pattern. For examples of border possibilities, look at "Summer" (page 34) and "Sunset Over the Sea" (page 65).

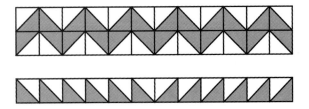

Other possibilities include putting the blocks on point, such as in "Noel" (page 32), or extending the quilt with a background that continues the pieced design in one color only, such as in "Noel" (page 32) and "Red Earth, Blue Sky – My Australia" (page 71).

While this book explores Four-patch blocks, they are not the only possibilities for using half-square triangles. For example, Carol Richards used combinations of six half-square triangle units for her quilt "Neon Lights Over Melbourne" (page 75).

To explore some of the design possibilities yourself, study the fifteen block patterns we have provided and the quilts we show you. Then, try drawing some of your own designs using the grid on page 80. Photocopy the gridded page, pick up a pencil and eraser and have some fun!

APPLYING FABRICS TO THE DESIGNS
Having chosen your two color families, how do you go about putting them into a design? The first step is to create at least sixty-four half-square triangle units (for construction techniques, see pages 18–23) with half of each square from one color and half from the other. As you put the triangles together, always keep the colors in their place in the design, but try to mix up the combinations as much as possible with regard to the tonal values and the type of prints. Put different tonal values together, such as darks with lights, mediums with darks, mediums with lights, and so on. Avoid putting light with light, medium with medium and dark with dark. The reason for avoiding these same tonal-value combinations is that they will make noticeable squares in the quilt. As you mix the tonal values, also be aware that if you put your lightest light next to your darkest dark, the juxtaposition will really emphasize both the lightness and darkness of each one. This can be avoided by pairing the very darkest and lightest prints with mediums.

Always try to mix up the style and scale of your prints, putting large prints with small prints, sparse prints with busy prints, spots with other patterns, and so on.

Having created lots of half-square triangle units, play with them to form different block designs. See four sample patterns opposite. As you arrange the half-square triangle units into patterns, make sure that you leave no spaces between the units, as any spaces will distract from the design. Put the units together spontaneously – don't agonise over every decision. Again, your aim is to mix up the colors, tonal values and prints as much as possible.

You will find that while there are lots of possibilities, one arrangement may work better than the others. You may have begun with a preconceived idea about which design you are going to make, but always be prepared to abandon it if a different design works better. Also, note that some possibilities work better on a bigger quilt rather than a smaller one, as the pattern may work better with more repeats.

Mix tonal values and prints when constructing the half-square triangle units.

Above: Four sample patterns created with half-square triangles in the same two color families.

Construction

There are many ways of making a half-square triangle unit, and you should use the method that suits your equipment, your fabric stash and your inclinations. But first, an important word about measurements.

STANDARD MEASUREMENTS

For most construction methods, triangles are cut from squares which are then cut in half on the diagonal to make two triangles. The square must therefore include the seam allowances around both triangles.

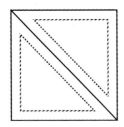

There are two approaches to the measurements for cutting the squares and the resultant triangles.

I Using standard seam allowances and sizes

The triangles are cut so that they are an exact finished size plus the standard seam allowances, which are 1/4" in imperial measurements and 7.5 mm in metric measurements (Margaret prefers this approach).

There are advantages to this approach if you want to add any other shapes to the quilt top, because other shapes are easy to cut and combine when the standard measurements are used. For example, see the border of small triangles on the quilt "Red Earth, Blue Sky – My Australia" on page 71. Also, any leftover triangles are ready to be used in another quilting project, if standard sizes are used.

If you wish to cut triangles that will be an exact finished size, then use the following guide to cutting sizes that include the standard seam allowances of 1/4" (7.5 mm):
For 4" (10 cm) triangles (finished size), cut squares 4 7/8" (12.5 cm).

For 3 1/2" (9 cm) triangles (finished size), cut squares 4 3/8" (11.5 cm).
For 3" (8 cm) triangles (finished size), cut squares 3 7/8" (10.5 cm).
For 2 1/2" (7 cm) triangles (finished size), cut squares 3 3/8" (9.5 cm).

2 Non-standard measurements

The other approach is to accept that you are making a One-patch quilt (that is, it will be made from the repetition of a single shape), and that therefore both the seam-allowance size and the exact size of the patch are not important (Judy prefers this approach). Note that there is only a difference in measurements if you are cutting in inches.

For this approach, cut the square 1" larger than the desired size of your finished triangles. The measurement is 1" because this measurement is very close to the 7/8" of the exact measurement. For example, if you want the finished size to be approximately 3", then cut squares 4". Any size seam allowance you prefer may be used. Some people like to use the width of the sewing machine foot, regardless of its measurement. Note that in this book the exact measurements are always given, so if you are working in imperial measurements and want to follow this other approach, add 1" to the size of the finished size of the triangle, and this will give you the size to cut the squares.

Whatever your approach to the size of your seam allowances, note that for accurate piecing it is necessary to maintain a consistent seam allowance within a project.

QUILT SIZES

It is also useful to know how the different sized half-square triangle units will make up into quilts, so a table of sizes for this purpose is given on page 19. Choose the size of half-square triangle unit you wish to use, then use the table to discover the length of multiple blocks placed side by side. Note that the blocks are Four-patch blocks (composed of four half-square triangle units).

Table of sizes

4" (10 cm) finished size of half-square triangle units
– block size 8" (20 cm)

× 4 blocks	=	32" (80 cm)
× 5 blocks	=	40" (100 cm)
× 6 blocks	=	48" (120 cm)
× 7 blocks	=	56" (140 cm)
× 8 blocks	=	64" (160 cm)
× 9 blocks	=	72" (180 cm)
× 10 blocks	=	80" (200 cm)

3¹/2" (9 cm) finished size of half-square triangle units
– block size 7" (18 cm)

× 4 blocks	=	28" (72 cm)
× 5 blocks	=	35" (90 cm)
× 6 blocks	=	42" (108 cm)
× 7 blocks	=	49" (126 cm)
× 8 blocks	=	56" (144 cm)
× 9 blocks	=	63" (162 cm)
× 10 blocks	=	70" (180 cm)
× 11 blocks	=	77" (198 cm)

3" (8 cm) finished size of half-square triangle units
– block size 6" (16 cm)

× 4 blocks	=	24" (64 cm)
× 5 blocks	=	30" (80 cm)
× 6 blocks	=	36" (96 cm)
× 7 blocks	=	42" (112 cm)
× 8 blocks	=	48" (128 cm)
× 9 blocks	=	54" (144 cm)
× 10 blocks	=	60" (160 cm)
× 11 blocks	=	66" (176 cm)
× 12 blocks	=	72" (192 cm)

2¹/2" (7 cm) finished size of half-square triangle units
– block size 5" (14 cm)

× 4 blocks	=	20" (56 cm)
× 5 blocks	=	25" (70 cm)
× 6 blocks	=	30" (84 cm)
× 7 blocks	=	35" (98 cm)
× 8 blocks	=	40" (112 cm)
× 9 blocks	=	45" (126 cm)
× 10 blocks	=	50" (140 cm)
× 11 blocks	=	55" (154 cm)
× 12 blocks	=	60" (168 cm)
× 13 blocks	=	65" (182 cm)
× 14 blocks	=	70" (196 cm)

METHODS FOR MAKING HALF-SQUARE TRIANGLE UNITS

The half-square triangle unit.

Included here are all the possible ways of making the half-square triangle units. Rotary cutting methods will be described first, because they are a fast and efficient way of cutting out half-square triangles. Then other techniques are covered, because not everyone likes to use a rotary cutter. (Note that the following is only a guide to methods for making the half-square triangle units – a general guide to rotary cutting techniques is given on pages 76–78.)

Rotary cutting squares from paired fabrics

This is Judy's favourite technique.

First, choose a fabric from each of your two color families. From each fabric, cut a rectangle that is approximately ¹/2" (2 cm) larger all around than two squares of your chosen size. For example, if your chosen size is 4" (10 cm) finished size, the squares need to be cut 4⁷/8" (12.5 cm), so the appropriate rectangle (larger than two squares together) will be about 5¹/2" × 10¹/2" (14.5 cm × 27 cm). Lay one of the rectangles on the ironing board, RIGHT SIDE UP, and spray evenly with spray starch. Place the other rectangle of fabric on top, RIGHT SIDE DOWN. Press well. The fabrics will now be lightly stuck together and will be very crisp and flat, ready for cutting.

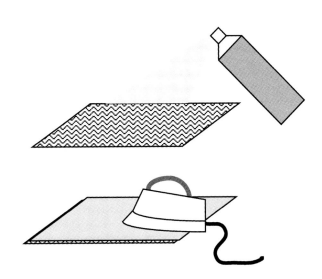

Using a rotary cutter, cut out two squares the required size, then cut each square in half along the diagonal to make four pairs of triangles.

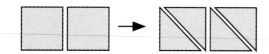

Handle the fabrics as little and as lightly as possible so that they remain stuck together. For example, rather than picking up the fabrics to make cuts, you may prefer to turn your cutting board around.

Stitch the triangles together with a 1/4" (7.5 mm) seam allowance (or the seam allowance of your choice if you are not following standard measurements). Press the triangles open, pressing to either the darker side or the side that will help make the block sit flat. Trim off the "ears" of seam allowance (Judy is most insistent that you always do this).

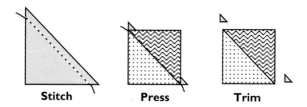

Stitch   **Press**   **Trim**

If you wish to use the fabrics again, cut out further rectangles, but pair them up with other fabrics in the quilt to create more variety.

Evaluation:

Positive   fabrics are cut in pairs ready for sewing

Negative   extra step of cutting out the rectangles

"ears" need to be cut off

Rotary cutting single triangles

This is Margaret's preferred technique.

Using the rotary cutter, cut strips the width of the squares in your chosen size. Cut only short strips of fabric, so that not too many triangles of one fabric are cut. Cut the strips into squares, then cut the squares across the diagonal to make half-square triangles. Fabrics can be cut in two or four layers to make cutting quicker.

Choosing one from each color family in your quilt, put triangles together into pairs, RIGHT SIDES TOGETHER.

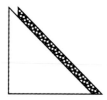

Sew the triangles together, using a 1/4" (7.5 mm) seam allowance.

Press the seam allowances toward the predominantly darker fabric or toward the side that will help make the block sit flat.

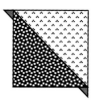

Trim away the "ears" of seam allowance, so that the square is actually all square.

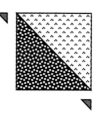

For efficient piecing and less waste of thread, chain-piece the triangles by first stacking them up in pairs, then feeding them through the machine without cutting the threads between each pair. Snip the pieced squares apart after stitching.

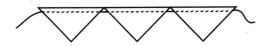

Evaluation:

Positive most economical with fabric
allows any fabric to be paired with any other

Negative "ears" need to be cut off

Working from squares

Cut squares of fabric using rotary cutting techniques. Arrange the squares together into pairs of the two colors in the quilt, RIGHT SIDES TOGETHER, with the lighter color on top.

Using a sharp pencil, or a chalk marker for dark fabrics, draw a diagonal line on the top square in each pair.

Sew down each side of the drawn line, using an accurate 1/4" (7.5 mm) seam allowance.

Cut down the drawn line, either with the rotary cutter or scissors. Press the squares open and trim away the "ears".

Evaluation:

Positive economical with fabric
avoids sewing along a cut bias edge

Negative "ears" need to be trimmed
involves the extra step of drawing line
across squares

Bias-strip method

Take four same-sized pieces of fabric, two from each of your color families. An ideal size is half of a "fat quarter" (sometimes called a "fat eighth") which is approximately 9" × 21" (23 cm × 54 cm), although other sizes can be used. Don't make the pieces too big as you will end up with too many of the same combination. Stack the fabrics, RIGHT SIDES UP, on your cutting board.

Align the 45° line marked on your ruler with the bottom edges of the stacked fabric. The edge of your ruler should now be on a 45° angle to the fabric. Move the ruler left or right until the distance from the bottom corner of the fabrics to the cutting edge of the ruler measures the same as the size of square you wish to cut.

Note: The size of the square you need to cut is the finished size of the half-square triangle unit plus 1/2" (1.5 cm) for seam allowances. For example, if you wish to cut 3 1/2" (9.5 cm) squares (for 3" (8 cm) finished size), this is the distance that should be measured from the corner.

Cut the fabric. You should now have a bias cut across one corner of the fabrics.

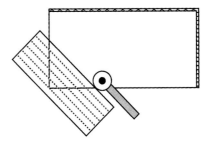

Measuring from the bias-cut edge, cut strips across the width of the fabric the measurement of the square. For example, for 3 1/2" (9.5 cm) squares, cut each strip 3 1/2" (9.5 cm) wide.

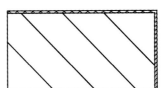

In each alternate pile of strips, rearrange the order of the fabrics so that the colors alternate and there is as much variety as possible.

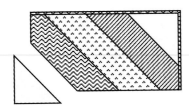

Sew the strips together to form the four new "rectangles", and press the seams to one side. Always begin sewing from the same side of the rectangle so that this edge will be even, but expect that the other edges will be uneven.

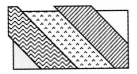

Using a small square ruler, cut squares from the pieced rectangles. Make the squares the desired size, with the diagonal seam lying on the diagonal of the square. It is easiest to begin cutting in a bottom corner and work systematically across. Each square will require two right-angled cuts. First, a right-angle cut to make two sides of the square and separate the shape from the rectangle. Second, the shape is flipped around for a second right-angle cut to make it square.

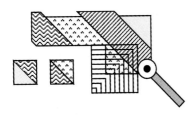

It is a good idea to cut two sets of four fabrics each, then mix up the strips from all eight fabrics to create even more combinations.

Evaluation:

Positive	most accurate of all techniques
	no "ears" to trim
	efficient time-wise
	excellent for small triangles
Negative	a little more fabric wasted than other methods
	not good for larger triangles

Drawing a grid

This is our least favourite method.

Take two same-sized pieces of fabric, one from each of your color families. An ideal size is a rectangle that is a little larger than two of your chosen size of squares, although other sizes can be used. Place the fabrics, RIGHT SIDES TOGETHER, on a flat surface.

Mark two squares on the top fabric, using either pencil or a thin chalk line. Make the squares the size required, including seam allowances. Draw diagonal lines across the squares.

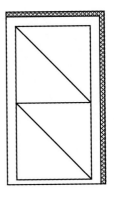

Sew down either side of each diagonal line, keeping an even seam allowance.

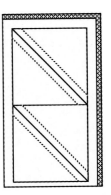

Cut along the marked lines with either scissors or a rotary cutter. Press the squares open. Check that the squares are accurate and re-trim them as required. Trim off the "ears".

Evaluation:

Positive   can be cut with either rotary cutter or scissors
avoids sewing on bias edges

Negative   extra step of drawing squares is required
less accurate than other methods and final
squares need re-trimming

In a variation of this technique, you can use commercially available printed papers that have the appropriate lines marked on them. Sew through the paper with the two fabrics stacked, RIGHT SIDES TOGETHER, beneath the paper. After sewing, cut the squares apart and rip the paper away.

Template for machine piecing

There are quilters who prefer not to use a rotary cutter but wish to machine-piece. In this case, the most accurate method is to prepare a template of the triangle, including the seam allowances. Use template plastic or firm, light cardboard as the template material. Draw a square of the size you require for your finished triangle, then draw a line from corner to corner across the diagonal, making two triangles. Measuring very carefully, draw a line exactly $1/4$" (7.5 mm) around one of the triangles. Cut out the triangle and label it with the size.

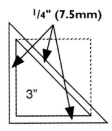

Place the template on the wrong side of the fabric and draw around the triangle using a sharp pencil. The shapes may be butted up next to each other. Cut out the triangles, then sew them together in pairs, trimming away the "ears" after pressing.

Evaluation:

Positive   suitable for those who prefer scissor cutting

Negative   time-consuming

Template sewing for hand-piecing

There are people who are either not in a situation to use a sewing machine or who just prefer to hand-piece. For hand-piecing, make a template from template plastic or firm, light cardboard. Draw a square the size you require for your finished triangle, then draw a line from corner to corner across the diagonal, making two triangles. Cut out one triangle and label it with its size.

Place the triangle on the wrong side of the fabric and mark around it with a sharp pencil. Note that this template does not include seam allowances, so leave a seam allowance around the marked line when you cut out each shape.

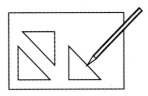

Pin the triangles together before sewing, aligning the marked lines by pinning the corners first.

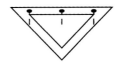

Sew on the marked line, using a small running stitch. Begin two stitches from the end, sew back into the corner, then sew along the line to its end. Finally, backtrack two stitches back along the line and finish off with a couple of backstitches.

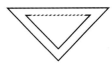

Evaluation:

Positive   portable, as cutting and sewing may be
done anywhere

Negative   time-consuming

PRESSING

We have suggested pressing the seam allowance of the half-square triangles toward either the darker of the two fabrics OR to the side that will make your block sit flat. The problem here is that when you begin making the half-square triangle units, you may not yet know which block will best suit your units. A tip is to only press enough blocks to try out the design possibilities and leave the remainder unpressed for the time being. Then, after you have chosen the block design, press the half-square triangles appropriately for the chosen block.

PIECING THE BLOCK

After the units of two half-square triangles are created, they are sewn together to make a Four-patch block. As already suggested, it is best to first try out different designs in order to make sure you have chosen the best design for your fabric combinations.

Having selected the block design, lay out the units in groups of four, with the units in their correct orientation.

At this point, it is also a good idea to think about how you will press the seam allowances in the block. Ideally you want the seam allowances to sit flat at seam junctions by being sewn in opposite directions. Plan how this might be possible with your particular block and press accordingly.

The sample block that we are using is the pattern of Block 1, which creates a chevron. Begin by choosing four half-square triangle units.

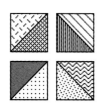

Pick up the upper two units, place them right sides together. Sew them together using whatever seam allowance you have maintained throughout.

Without snipping the thread, pick up the other two units, place them right sides together and sew the seam.

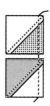

Press the seam allowances to one side, making the seam allowances of the upper two units go in the opposite direction of the lower two units.

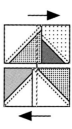

Sew the two sets of units together and press the seam to one side.

It is possible to chain-piece by sewing the units together into pairs then cutting the thread after every second pair. Press the seam allowances as above, then sew the remaining seam for each block, again chain-piecing then snipping the blocks apart.

ASSEMBLING THE QUILT TOP

After making the blocks, it is important to lay them out in the arrangement you have chosen. Again, at this stage it is best to play with the blocks to investigate the possibilities. If possible, work on a design wall (a large board covered with felt or other napped fabric, such as white flannel). Alternatively, you can use a sheet pinned to a curtain or wall, or else lay out the blocks in a clear space on the floor. Even a bed can be used as a temporary layout space.

Lay out the blocks in a spontaneous way, trying to mix the colors, tonal values and varieties of prints as much as possible. If any areas bother you, move the blocks around until the whole pleases you. Looking through a reducing glass or a camera can help you spot problem areas.

After the blocks have been laid out in their final positions, sew them together into rows. Press the seams in alternate rows in opposite directions. However, note that it will not always be possible to have all the seams alternating at every seam junction on the sides of the blocks. Accept that some junctions will have all the seams going in one direction, but work to make them go alternately wherever possible, re-pressing some seams if necessary.

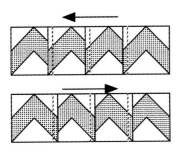

Sew the rows together to make the center of the quilt. The seam allowances at the junctions of the blocks should lie neatly in opposite directions (even if junctions of seam allowances at the sides of the blocks don't).

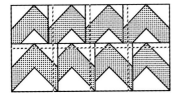

Borders

Add a border or borders as suits the quilt design and your chosen fabrics. Look at the quilt projects and the gallery of quilts to give you lots of ideas. Some of the possibilities are:

- Adding a single outer border
- Adding one (or more) narrow border strips in an accent color to the outer border
- Adding pieced corners
- Piecing a border with triangles
- Piecing a border using other shapes

When adding borders, always measure the quilt top through the center to determine the lengths required. First measure the quilt length through its center. Cut the border strips to this length. Mark the centers of both the strips and the sides of the quilt top with pins (pin-mark). Sew the strips to the sides of the quilt top, matching the pin marks.

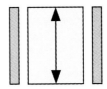

Measure the width of the quilt top through its center, including the newly added strips at both sides. Pin-mark the strips and quilt top as before, then add the top and bottom border strips.

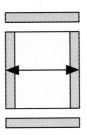

To add a border with corner squares, measure the quilt length and width through its center. Cut the border strips to these measurements. Cut or piece the corner squares to the width of the border strips. Sew the squares to the ends of the top and bottom border strips. Pin-mark the centers of the quilt top and the strips. Sew the side border strips to the quilt top, then the top and bottom strips, matching the pin marks.

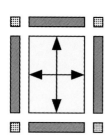

To make mitered corners, first cut border strips so that they are the length of the quilt center plus twice the width of the border plus 1" (2.5 cm). Pin-mark each strip in the center and at the corners of the quilt top.

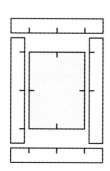

Stitch the border strips to the quilt, matching the pin marks to the center of the quilt and the corners and stitching to only 1/4" (or the size of your seam allowance) from the edge of the quilt at the corners.

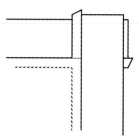

Working on each border strip in turn, mark a 45° angle from the corner point where you stopped stitching. Fold the quilt so that the border strips are parallel. Pin the borders together, matching the marked lines. Sew along the marked lines and trim away the excess fabric. Press these seams open.

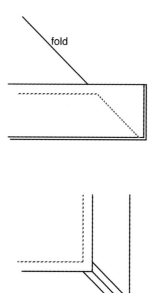

fold

LAYERING AND QUILTING

Cut the batting and backing so that they are 4" (10 cm) larger than the quilt top. The backing may have to be pieced together to make the appropriate size.

Working on a large space, such as a large table or the floor, spread out the backing, right side down. Smooth the batting over the backing. Finally, lay the quilt top over the batting, right side up.

Thread-basting is preferable for hand-quilting, while pin-basting using safety pins is preferable for machine-quilting. Baste or pin the quilt at 4" (10 cm) intervals or less. When using safety pins, use a two-step approach. First, pin and leave the pins open. When they are all in place, close all the pins. This approach avoids rumpling the layers while pinning.

Hand-quilt or machine-quilt, as desired. These scrap quilts lend themselves to simple grid-quilting of either straight or wavy lines. Simple free-motion quilting is also a possibility.

For machine-quilting, the quilt will need to be rolled up to fit under the machine. Roll and re-roll the quilt as required to allow you to quilt across the surface. Chalk can be used to mark straight lines.

Use a thread for quilting that will blend into the colors of the quilt, or else use clear, monofilament thread. Monofilament thread should only be used through the needle.

A walking foot will help the layers move smoothly through the machine.

Hand-quilting is a simple running stitch going through all three layers of the quilt. Aim for even stitches rather than very small ones. Use a quilting frame or hoop to support the quilt, and protect your fingers with a thimble or other protector. Use a quilting thread and a between needle for the stitching. Mark quilting lines with chalk or masking tape. Do not leave the tape on the quilt when you are not working on it, as it can leave a mark.

BINDING

Cut 2 1/2" (7 cm) wide strips for the binding for a 3/8" (1 cm) finished size or 3" (8 cm) wide strips for a 1/2" (1.5 cm) finished size. Join strips as necessary to achieve the length (or lengths) required, using diagonal seams to distribute the bulk of the seam allowances. Press the strips in half lengthwise.

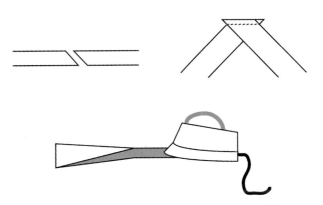

There are two ways of sewing on the binding. The first method, which Judy uses, is to make one long length of binding and sew it to the back of the quilt, stitching and folding it to make mitered corners and folding in one end neatly to make a smooth join. The binding is then folded to the front of the quilt and machine stitched in place.

The second method, which Margaret prefers, is to join the binding to the quilt in a similar way as you do the borders. Cut the binding into four lengths which are carefully measured so that they are the same as the center measurement of the quilt. The prepared binding strips are sewn to the top of the quilt, with the corners either mitered or square. The binding is then folded to the back of the quilt and hand-sewn in place.

The Quilts

Now we come to the best part of the book – the quilts. The joy of Spectacular Scraps is in making the quilts. There are many stages of the process to enjoy: choosing your two color families, gathering together the fabrics (this is a lot of fun, whether you are sorting through your fabric stash or going on an expedition to find more fabrics), cutting out the triangles, sewing the blocks together, then the best part of all – seeing the quilt grow and develop before your eyes.

In this book, there are fifteen quilt projects for your inspiration and a further sixteen quilts pictured in the gallery. We have used lots of different color combinations and a wide variety of block designs to show just some of the many, many possibilities which come from our approach to making scrap quilts. We hope you will use ideas from these quilts to make your very own spectacular scrap quilts.

Swizzle

BY JUDY HOOWORTH

YOU WILL NEED

**Note: Fabric quantities
are calculated on 44"
(112 cm) wide fabric.**

- 1¼ yds (1.2 m) of
  **black-and-white print
  fabric for the outer
  border**
- approximately ¾ yd
  (70 cm) total of
  **assorted yellow
  print fabrics**
- approximately ¾ yd
  (70 cm) total of
  **assorted black print
  fabrics**
- ¼ yd (25 cm) of
  **orange print fabric for
  the inner border**
- 48" x 48" (125 cm x
  125 cm) piece of
  batting
- 1¾ yds (160 cm) of
  fabric for the backing
- ½ yd (50 cm) of
  **yellow-and-black
  (or yellow-and-navy)
  striped fabric for
  the binding**
- usual cutting, sewing
  and quilting supplies

Finished size: 44" x 44" (109 cm x 109 cm)

Block design
Make sixteen

Group of four blocks

CONSTRUCTION

1 Using the method of your choice (see
   pages 18–23), make sixty-four half-
   square triangle units, 4" (10 cm) finished
   size, combining the yellow and black
   print fabrics. If you are rotary cutting the
   triangles, cut 4⅞" (12.5 cm) squares,
   cutting thirty-two squares each from the
   yellow and black print fabrics.

2 Assemble the half-square triangle units
   into sixteen blocks, following the block
   diagram.

3 Arrange the blocks into four rows of
   four blocks each, following the quilt
   diagram. Join the blocks into rows, then
   join the rows to make the center of the
   quilt top.

For the borders

1 From the orange print fabric for the
   inner border, cut four strips, each
   1½" (4 cm) wide. Always measuring the
   quilt top through its center to find the
   lengths required, trim and sew two strips
   to the sides of the quilt top, then trim
   and sew the remaining two strips to the
   top and bottom.

2 From the black-and-white print fabric
   for the outer border and cutting down
   the length of the fabric, cut four 5½"
   (13.5 cm) wide strips. Join the outer
   border to the quilt top in the same
   way as the inner border.

TO FINISH

1 Piece the backing fabric as required to
   make a 48" x 48" (120 cm x 120 cm)
   square.

2 Layer the backing, batting and quilt top.
   Pin-baste or thread-baste layers together.

3 Quilt as desired.

4 From the yellow striped fabric for the
   binding, cut five 3" (8 cm) wide strips.
   Join them to achieve the length required
   and bind the quilt.

"Swizzle" by Judy Hooworth
44" x 44" (109 cm x 109 cm)
Block design 1

Noel

BY MARGARET ROLFE

YOU WILL NEED

Note: Fabric quantities are calculated for 44" (112 cm) wide fabric.

- 2 yds (1.7 m) of red Christmas print fabric for the border and binding
- approximately 1 1/2 yds (1.4 m) total of assorted red Christmas print fabrics
- approximately 1 3/4 yds (1.6 m) total of assorted green Christmas print fabrics
- 71" x 71" (176 cm x 176 cm) piece of batting
- 4 yds (3.6 m) of fabric for the backing
- usual cutting, sewing and quilting supplies

Finished size: 67" (166 cm) square

Block designs

A (R/G)
Make 16

B (G/G)
Make 8

C (R/G)
Make 16

D (R/G)
Make 20

Group of four blocks

Quilt Assembly Diagram

CONSTRUCTION

1 Using the method of your choice (see pages 18–23), make a total of 180 half-square triangle units, 4" (10 cm) finished size, making 100 in the red-and-green (R/G) color combination and eighty in the green-and-green (G/G) color combination. Cut an additional forty triangles from the assorted red print fabrics. For rotary cutting the triangles, cut 4 7/8" (12.5 cm) squares, cutting seventy squares from the red prints and eighty squares from the green prints.

2 Assemble the half-square triangle units into blocks and half blocks, following the block designs, making sixteen A blocks, eight B blocks, sixteen C blocks and twenty D half blocks (for the edge).

3 To make quilt center, arrange the blocks, on the diagonal as shown in the Quilt Assembly Diagram.

4 Sewing the rows on the diagonal, sew the blocks into rows, then join the rows to make the center of the quilt top. Stay-stitch around the edge of the quilt center, to stabilize the bias edges.

For the borders:

1 From the red print fabric for the border, and cutting lengthwise down the fabric, cut four 5 1/2" (13.5 cm) wide strips.

2 Following the method for making borders with mitered corners on page 26, add the borders to the quilt.

TO FINISH

1 Cut the backing fabric into two equal lengths and join the lengths side by side. Trim to make a 71" (176 cm) square.

2 Layer the backing, batting and quilt top. Pin-baste or thread-baste the layers together.

3 Quilt in a grid of diagonal lines.

4 From the remainder of the red print fabric, cut four 2 1/2" (7 cm) wide strips for the binding. Bind the quilt.

"Noel" by Margaret Rolfe
67" x 67" (166 cm x 166 cm)
Block design 7

Summer

BY JUDY HOOWORTH

YOU WILL NEED

Note: Fabric quantities are calculated for 44" (112 cm) wide fabric.

- approximately 3¹/₂ yds (3.2 m) total of assorted yellow print fabrics
- approximately 4³/₄ yds (4.3 m) total of assorted orange print fabrics
- approximately 2¹/₂ yds (2.3 m) total of assorted red print fabrics
- 92" x 92" (230 cm x 230 cm) piece of batting
- 7³/₄ yds (7 m) of fabric for the backing
- 1 yd (80 cm) of orange print fabric for the binding
- usual cutting, sewing and quilting supplies

Finished size: 88" (220 cm) square

Quilt Assembly Diagram

Block A design (Y/O)
Make 64

Block B design (R/O/Y)
Make 16

Block B design reverse (R/O/Y)
Make 16

Block C design (R/O/Y)
Make 4

Block D design (R/O)
Make 40

CONSTRUCTION

1 Using the method of your choice (see pages 18–23), make a total of 484 half-square triangle units, 4" (10 cm) finished size, making 256 in the yellow-and-orange (Y/O) combination, 36 in the red-and-yellow (R/Y) combination, and 192 in the red-and-orange (R/O) combination. For rotary cutting the triangles, cut 4⁷/₈" (12.5 cm) squares, cutting 146 squares from the yellow print fabrics, 224 squares from the orange print fabrics, and 114 squares from the red print fabrics.

2 Assemble the half-square triangle units into blocks and half blocks, following the block designs, making sixty-four A blocks, sixteen B blocks, sixteen reverse B blocks and four D corner blocks. Four red/orange half-square triangle units will remain to complete the corners.

3 Arrange the A blocks into eight rows of eight blocks each, as shown in the Quilt Assembly Diagram.

4 Sew the blocks into rows, then join the rows to make the center of the quilt top.

For the borders:

1 Arrange the remaining blocks, half blocks and four half-square triangle units to make the borders, as shown in the quilt assembly diagram.

2 Join the blocks for the side borders, and sew them to the sides of the quilt top. Join the blocks for the top and bottom borders, and join them to the quilt top.

TO FINISH

1 Cut the backing fabric into three equal lengths and join the lengths side by side. Trim to make a 92" (230 cm) square.

2 Layer the backing, batting and quilt top. Pin-baste or thread-baste the layers together.

3 Quilt as desired.

4 From the fabric for the binding, cut nine 3" (8 cm) wide strips. Join the strips to achieve the length required. Bind the quilt.

"Summer" by Judy Hooworth, quilted by
The Patchwork Shop, Gold Creek Village, Canberra
88" x 88" (220 cm x 220 cm)
Block designs 1 and 4

Gathering Rosebuds

BY MARGARET ROLFE

YOU WILL NEED

Note: Fabric quantities are calculated for 44" (112 cm) wide fabric.

- **2³/4 yds (2.4 m) of blue-and-pink floral print fabric for the border and binding**
- **approximately 4¹/4 yds (4 m) total of assorted blue floral print fabrics**
- **approximately 4¹/4 yds (4 m) total of assorted pink floral print fabrics**
- **95" x 95" (238 cm x 238 cm) piece of batting**
- **8 yds (7.2 m) of fabric for the backing**
- **usual cutting, sewing and quilting supplies**

Finished size: 91" (228 cm) square

Block design
Make 100

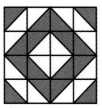

Group of four blocks

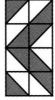

Half of group of four blocks

CONSTRUCTION

1 Using the method of your choice (see pages 18–23), make 400 half-square triangle units, 4" (10 cm) finished size, from the assorted blue and pink print fabrics. For rotary cutting the triangles, cut 4⁷/8" (12.5 cm) squares, cutting 200 squares each from the blue and the pink print fabrics.

2 Assemble the half-square triangle units into 100 blocks, following the block design.

3 Arrange the blocks into ten rows of ten blocks each, as shown in the quilt diagram. Note that the sides of the quilt are formed with halves of the group of four blocks.

4 Sew the blocks into rows, then join the rows to make the center of the quilt top.

For the borders:

1 From blue-and-pink print fabric for the border, and cutting down the length of the fabric, cut four 6" (15.5 cm) wide strips.

2 Always measuring the quilt through the center to find the lengths required, trim and sew two strips to the sides of the quilt, then trim and sew the two remaining strips to the top and bottom.

TO FINISH

1 Cut the backing fabric into three equal lengths and join the lengths side by side. Trim to make a 95" (238 cm) square.

2 Layer the backing, batting and quilt top. Pin-baste or thread-baste the layers together.

3 Quilt as desired.

4 From the remainder of the blue-and-pink print fabric, and cutting down the length of the fabric, cut four 3" (8 cm) wide strips for the binding. Bind the quilt.

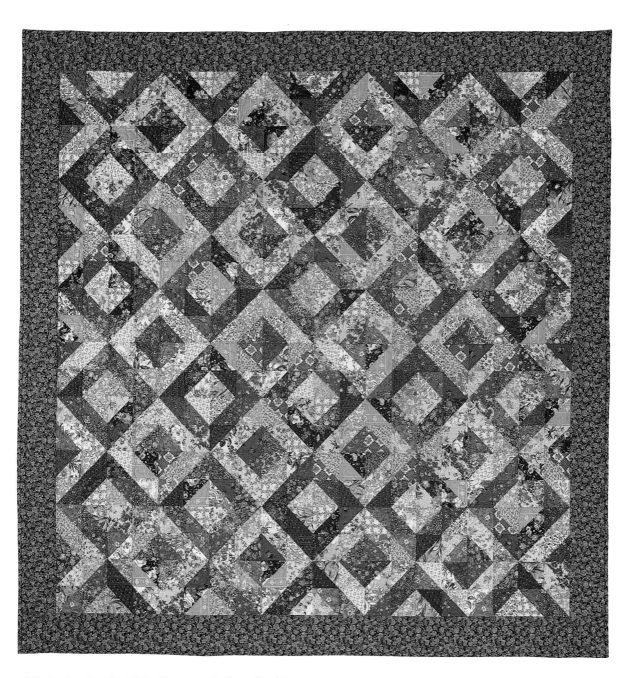

"Gathering Rosebuds" by Margaret Rolfe, quilted by
The Patchwork Shop, Gold Creek Village, Canberra
91" x 91" (228 cm x 228 cm)
Block design 4

Bonjour Paris

BY MARGARET ROLFE

YOU WILL NEED

Note: Fabric quantities are calculated for 44" (112 cm) wide fabric.

- 2¹/2 yds (2.3 m) of blue-and-yellow print fabric for the border
- approximately 3¹/2 yds (3.2 m) total of assorted blue print fabrics
- approximately 3¹/2 yds (3.2 m) total of assorted yellow print fabrics
- 87" x 87" (224 cm x 224 cm) piece of batting
- 7¹/2 yds (7 m) of fabric for the backing
- 1 yd (80 cm) of blue print fabric for the binding
- usual cutting, sewing and quilting supplies

Finished size: 83" (214 cm) square

Block A design
Make 64

Block B design
Make 17

CONSTRUCTION

1 Using the method of your choice (see pages 18–23), make 324 half-square triangle units, 3¹/2" (9 cm) finished size, combining the assorted yellow and the blue print fabrics. For rotary cutting the triangles, cut 4³/8" (11.5 cm) squares, cutting 162 squares each from the assorted yellow and blue print fabrics.

2 Assemble the half-square triangle units into sixty-four A blocks and seventeen B blocks, following the block designs.

3 Arrange the blocks into nine rows of nine blocks each as shown in the quilt diagram.

4 Sew the blocks into rows, then join the rows to make the center of the quilt top.

For the borders:

1 From the yellow-and-blue print fabric for the border, and cutting lengthways down the fabric, cut four 10¹/2" (27.5 cm) wide strips.

2 Following the method for making borders with mitered corners on page 26, add the border strips to the quilt.

TO FINISH

1 Cut the backing fabric into three equal lengths and join the lengths side by side. Trim to make an 87" (224 cm) square.

2 Layer the backing, batting and quilt top. Pin-baste or thread-baste the layers together.

3 Quilt as desired.

4 From the blue print fabric for the binding, cut nine 3" (8 cm) wide strips. Join the strips to achieve the length required. Bind the quilt.

"Bonjour Paris" by Margaret Rolfe, quilted by
The Patchwork Shop, Gold Creek Village, Canberra
83" x 83" (214 cm x 214 cm)
Block designs 1 and 2

Octopus' Garden

BY JUDY HOOWORTH

YOU WILL NEED

Note: Fabric quantities are calculated for 44" (112 cm) wide fabric.

- approximately 1 1/2 yds (1.4 m) total of assorted orange print fabrics
- approximately 1 1/2 yds (1.4 m) total of assorted purple print fabrics
- 3/4 yd (60 cm) of orange print fabric for the top and left-hand borders
- 3/4 yd (60 cm) of purple print fabric for the bottom and right-hand borders
- 62" x 62" (154 cm x 154 cm) piece of batting
- 3 1/2 yds (3.1 m) of fabric for the backing
- 3/4 yd (60 cm) of orange striped fabric for the binding
- usual cutting, sewing and quilting supplies

Finished size: 58" (144 cm) square

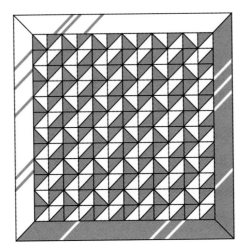

Block design
Make 36

CONSTRUCTION

1 Using the method of your choice (see pages 18–23), make 144 half-square triangle units, 4" (10 cm) finished size, combining the assorted orange and the purple prints. For rotary cutting the triangles, cut 4 7/8" (12.5 cm) squares, cutting seventy-two squares each from the orange and the purple prints.
2 Assemble the half-square triangle units into thirty-six blocks, following the block design.
3 Arrange the blocks into six rows of six blocks each, as shown in the quilt diagram.
4 Sew the blocks into rows, then join the rows to make the center of the quilt top.

For the borders:

1 From the orange print fabric for the top and left-hand border, and cutting across the width of the fabric, cut four 5 1/4" (13.5 cm) wide strips.
2 From the purple print fabric for the bottom and right-hand border, and cutting across the width of the fabric, cut four 5 1/4" (13.5 cm) wide strips.
3 From the assorted orange print fabrics, cut eight 3/4" x 8" (2 cm x 20 cm) strips. From the assorted purple print fabrics, cut seven 3/4" x 8" (2 cm x 20 cm) strips.
4 Lay out the quilt in a clear space. Note that each side of the quilt will require two of the strips of border print, with the orange strips going to the top and left of the quilt and the purple strips going to the bottom and right of the quilt. Lay out one orange border strip next to the quilt top, leaving 8" (20 cm) at the end for a mitered corner. Pin-mark the border where the first diagonal strip will go, following the quilt diagram. Cut the border at 45° from this pin mark, cutting the angle in the direction shown. Select an appropriate narrow purple strip and sew it into the border. Press flat. Repeat this pin-marking, cutting and sewing for each diagonal strip down the length of the border, introducing the second strip of border fabric when the first strip runs out. Leave 8" (20 cm) at the end of the border for the mitered corner. Repeat this process for the other three borders, changing from the orange border (with purple diagonal strips) to the purple border (with orange diagonal strips) as shown in the quilt diagram.
5 Following the method for making borders with mitered corners on page 26, add the borders to the quilt.

TO FINISH

1 Cut the backing fabric into two equal lengths and join the lengths side by side. Trim to make a 62" (154 cm) square.

2 Layer the backing, batting and quilt top. Pin-baste or thread-baste the layers together.

3 Quilt as desired.

4 From the orange striped fabric for the binding, cut six 3" (8 cm) wide strips. Join the strips to achieve the length required. Bind the quilt.

"Octopus' Garden" by Judy Hooworth
58" x 58" (144 cm x 144 cm)
Block design 6

Black Opal

BY MARGARET ROLFE

YOU WILL NEED

Note: Fabric quantities are calculated for 44" (112 cm) wide fabric.

- 2 yds (2 m) of black print fabric for the border and binding
- approximately 3½ yds (3.2 m) total of assorted purple print fabrics
- approximately 3½ yds (3.2 m) total of assorted black print fabrics
- 64" x 84" (174 cm x 230 cm) piece of batting
- 3¾ yds (3.5 m) of fabric for the backing
- usual cutting, sewing and quilting supplies

Finished size: 60" x 80" (164 cm x 220 cm)

Block design
Make 140

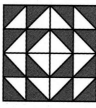

Group of four blocks

CONSTRUCTION

1 Using the method of your choice (see pages 18–23), make 560 half-square triangle units, 2½" (7 cm) finished size, combining the assorted purple and black prints. For rotary cutting the triangles, cut 3⅜" (9.5 cm) squares, cutting 280 squares each from the purple and the black print fabrics.

2 Assemble the half-square triangle units into 140 blocks. following the block design.

3 Arrange the blocks into fourteen rows of ten blocks each as shown in the quilt diagram.

4 Sew the blocks into rows, then join the rows to make the center of the quilt top.

For the borders:

1 From the black print fabric for the border, and cutting down the length of the fabric, cut four 5½" (13.5 cm) wide strips.

2 Always measuring the quilt through the center to find the lengths required, trim and sew two strips to the sides of the quilt, then trim and sew the two remaining strips to the top and bottom.

TO FINISH

1 Cut the backing fabric into two equal lengths and join the lengths side by side. Trim to make a rectangle 64" x 84" (174 cm x 230 cm).

2 Layer the backing, batting and quilt top. Pin-baste or thread-baste the layers together.

3 Quilt in grid of wavy diagonal lines.

4 From the remainder of the black print fabric, cut five 2½" (7 cm) wide strips. Join the strips to achieve the length required. Bind the quilt.

"Black Opal" by Margaret Rolfe
60" x 80" (164 cm x 220 cm)
Block design 12

Rainforest Rhythms

BY JUDY HOOWORTH

YOU WILL NEED

Note: Fabric quantities are calculated for 44" (112 cm) wide fabric.

- approximately 2³/4 yds (2.5 m) total of assorted black print fabrics
- approximately 2³/4 yds (2.5 m) total of assorted green print fabrics
- ¹/2 yd (50 cm) of green print fabric for the first border
- ¹/4 yd (30 cm) of bright green print fabric for the second border
- 2¹/4 yds (2.1 m) of black-and-green print fabric for the third border
- 83" x 83" (209 cm x 209 cm) piece of batting
- 5 yds (4.3 m) of fabric for the backing
- ³/4 yd (70 cm) of black-and-white striped fabric for the binding
- usual cutting, sewing and quilting supplies

Finished size: 79" (199 cm) square

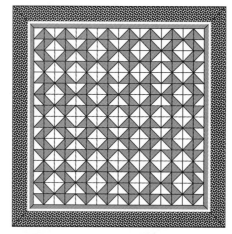

Block design
Make 32

Block design reverse
Make 32

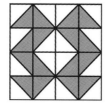

Group of four blocks

CONSTRUCTION

1 Using the method of your choice (see pages 18–23), make 256 half-square triangle units, 4" (10 cm) finished size, combining the assorted green and black print fabrics. For rotary cutting the triangles, cut 4⁷/8" (12.5 cm) squares, cutting 128 squares from each of the green and black print fabrics.

2 Assemble the half-square triangle units into thirty-two blocks and thirty-two reverse blocks, following the block designs.

3 Arrange the blocks into eight rows of eight blocks each, as shown in the quilt diagram.

4 Sew the blocks into rows, then join the rows to make the center of the quilt top.

For the borders:

1 From the green fabric for the first border, cut eight 2" (5.5 cm) wide strips. Join the strips in pairs, end-to-end, to achieve the required length.

2 From the bright green fabric for the second border, cut eight 1" (3 cm) wide strips. Join the strips in pairs, end-to-end, to achieve the required length.

3 From the black fabric for the third border, and cutting lengthwise down the fabric, cut four 6" (15.5 cm) wide strips.

4 Join the border strips together in their correct order.

5 Following the method for making borders with mitered corners (see page 26), add the border strips to the quilt.

TO FINISH

1 Cut the backing fabric into two equal lengths and join the lengths side by side. Trim to make an 83" (209 cm) square.

2 Layer the backing, batting and quilt top. Pin-baste or thread-baste the layers together.

3 Quilt as desired.

4 From the striped fabric for the binding, cut eight 3" (8 cm) wide strips. Join the strips to achieve the length required. Bind the quilt.

"Rainforest Rhythms" by Judy Hooworth
79" x 79" (199 cm x 199 cm)
Block design 10

Lavender's Green

BY MARGARET ROLFE

YOU WILL NEED

Note: Fabric quantities are calculated for 44" (112 cm) wide fabric.

- 2¹/4 yds (2 m) of lavender print fabric for the outer border
- approximately 1³/4 yds (1.7 m) total of assorted lavender print fabrics
- approximately 1³/4 yds (1.7 m) total of assorted green print fabrics
- ¹/2 yd (30 cm) of green print fabric for the inner border
- 58" x 76" (151 cm x 199 cm) piece of batting
- 3¹/4 yds (3.1 m) of fabric for the backing
- ³/4 yd (60 cm) of lavender print fabric for the binding
- usual cutting, sewing and quilting supplies

Finished size: 54" x 72" (141 cm x 189 cm)

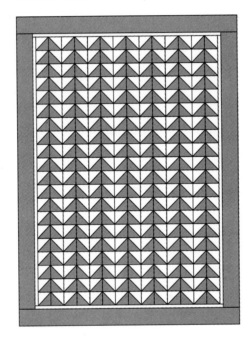

Block design
Make 70

CONSTRUCTION

1 Using the method of your choice (see pages 18–23), make 280 half-square triangle units, 3" (8 cm) finished size, combining the assorted lavender and green print fabrics. For rotary cutting the triangles, cut 3⁷/8" (10.5 cm) squares, cutting 140 squares each from the lavender and the green fabrics.

2 Assemble the half-square triangle units into seventy blocks following the block design.

3 Arrange the blocks into ten rows of seven blocks each, as shown in the quilt diagram.

4 Sew the blocks into rows, then join the rows to make the center of the quilt top.

For the borders:

1 From the green print fabric for the inner border, and cutting across the width of the fabric, cut six 1¹/2" (4 cm) wide strips.

2 Cut two strips in half. Join each half to one of the remaining four strips. Always measuring the quilt through the center to find the lengths required, trim and sew two strips to the sides of the quilt, then trim and sew the remaining two strips to the top and bottom.

3 From the fabric for the outer border, and cutting down the length of the fabric, cut four 5¹/2" (13.5 cm) wide strips. Measure and attach this border as for the inner border.

TO FINISH

1 Cut the backing fabric into two equal lengths and join the lengths side by side. Trim to make a rectangle 58" x 76" (151 cm x 199 cm).

2 Layer the backing, batting and quilt top. Pin-baste or thread-baste the layers together.

3 Quilt in a grid of diagonal lines.

4 From the fabric for the binding, cut seven 2¹/2" (7 cm) wide strips. Join the strips to achieve the length required. Bind the quilt.

"Lavender's Green" by
Margaret Rolfe
54" x 72" (141 cm x 189 cm)
Block design 8

Summer Peaches

BY MARGARET ROLFE

YOU WILL NEED

Note: Fabric quantities are calculated for 44" (112 cm) wide fabric.

- **2¹/₂ yds (2.5 m) of peach-and-blue print fabric for the third border and binding**
- **approximately 2¹/₂ yds (2.4 m) total of assorted peach print fabrics**
- **approximately 2¹/₂ yds (2.4 m) total of assorted blue print fabrics**
- **1 yd (90 cm) of blue print fabric for the second border**
- **¹/₂ yd (40 cm) of peach print fabric for the first border**
- **73" x 97" (188 cm x 252 cm) piece of batting**
- **5¹/₂ yds (5.1 m) of fabric for the backing**
- **usual cutting, sewing and quilting supplies**

Finished size: 68¹/₂" x 92¹/₂" (178 cm x 242 cm)

Block design
Make 96

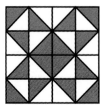

Group of four blocks

CONSTRUCTION

1 Using the method of your choice (see pages 18–23), make 384 half-square triangle units, 3" (8 cm) finished size, combining the assorted peach and blue print fabrics. For rotary cutting the triangles, cut 3⁷/₈" (10.5 cm) squares, cutting 192 squares each from the peach fabrics and blue fabrics.

2 Assemble the half-square triangle units into ninety-six blocks, following the block design.

3 Arrange the blocks into twelve rows of eight blocks each. Sew the blocks into rows, then join the rows to make the center of the quilt top.

For the borders:

1 From the fabric for the first border, and cutting across the width of the fabric, cut seven 1³/₄" (4.5 cm) wide strips. Cut one strip in half, then join one of the halves to each of two other strips. Join the remaining four strips into pairs.

2 Always measuring the quilt through the center to find the lengths required, trim and sew the two longer strips to the sides of the quilt, then trim and sew the two shorter strips to the top and bottom.

3 From the blue fabric for the second border, and cutting across the width of the fabric, cut seven 4¹/₂" (11.5 cm) wide strips. Cut one strip in half, then join one half to each of two other strips. Join the remaining four strips into two pairs. Measure and attach this border as for the inner border.

4 From peach-and-blue fabric for the third border, and cutting down the length of the fabric, cut four 5¹/₂" (13.5 cm) wide strips. Join this border to the quilt as before.

TO FINISH

1 Cut the backing fabric into two equal lengths. Join then trim the lengths to make a rectangle 73" x 97" (188 cm x 252 cm).

2 Layer the backing, batting and quilt top. Pin-baste or thread-baste the layers together.

3 Quilt in grid of diagonal wavy lines.

4 From the remaining peach-and-blue print fabric, cut four 3" (8 cm) wide strips for the binding. Bind the quilt.

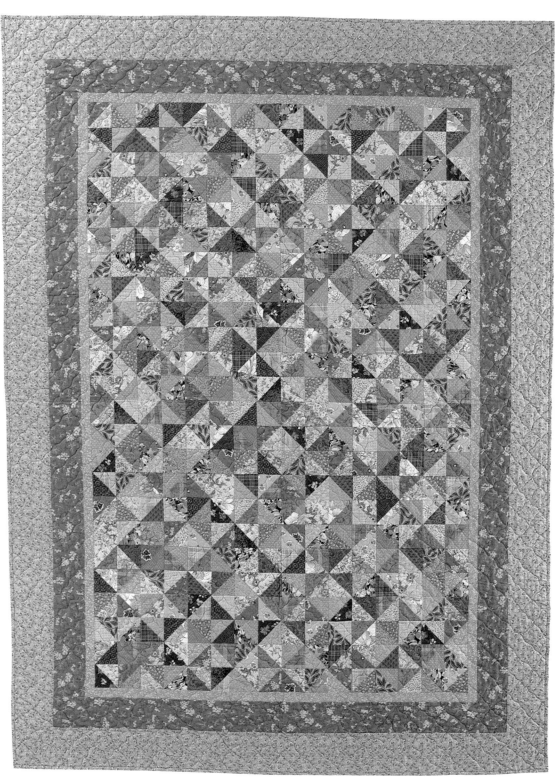

"Summer Peaches" by
Margaret Rolfe
68¹/₂" x 92¹/₂" (178 cm x 242 cm)
Block design 3

Teddy Bears' Picnic

BY MARGARET ROLFE

YOU WILL NEED

Note: Fabric quantities are calculated for 44" (112 cm) wide fabric.

- 1 1/4 yds (1 m) of two-color feature fabric for the border and pieced center (This quantity assumes a print that reads one way – if the feature print is non-directional, only 1 yd (80 cm) is required.)
- approximately 1/2 yd (50 cm) total of assorted prints in the first color of the feature print
- approximately 1/2 yd (50 cm) total of assorted prints in the second color (or contrast color) of the feature print
- 39" x 39" (102 cm x 102 cm) piece of batting
- 1 1/4 yds (1.1 m) of fabric for the backing
- 1/2 yd (50 cm) of fabric for the binding
- usual cutting, sewing and quilting supplies

Finished size: 35" (92 cm) square

CONSTRUCTION

1 From the feature fabric, cut two 6" (15.5 cm) wide strips, cutting across the width of the fabric. Cut two more 6" (15.5 cm) wide strips, cutting down the length of the remaining fabric. If using a non-directional print, cut four strips across the width of the fabric. Set these strips aside for the borders of the quilt.

2 Using the method of your choice (see pages 18–23), make a total of sixty-four half-square triangle units, 3" (8 cm) finished size. Make forty-eight units combining the first and second color prints, and sixteen units that combine the feature print and an assortment of the second-color prints. If you are rotary cutting the triangles, cut 3 7/8" (10.5 cm) squares, cutting eight squares from the feature fabric, twenty-four squares from the first-color prints and thirty-two squares from the second-color prints.

When you cut along the diagonals of the squares of feature fabric, cut four squares with the diagonal one way and four squares with the diagonal the opposite way.

3 Arrange the half-square triangle units into eight rows of eight units, distributing the half-square triangles of feature fabric around the quilt as shown in the quilt diagram.

4 Join the units into rows, then join the rows to make the center of the quilt top.

For the borders:

Using the already-cut border strips, and always measuring the quilt top through its center to find the lengths required, trim and sew two strips to the sides of the quilt. Trim and sew the remaining two strips to the top and bottom.

TO FINISH

1 Layer the backing, batting and quilt top. Pin-baste or thread-baste the layers together.

2 Quilt in a diamond pattern following the piecing.

3 From the fabric for the binding, cut four 2 1/2" (7 cm) wide strips for the binding. Bind the quilt.

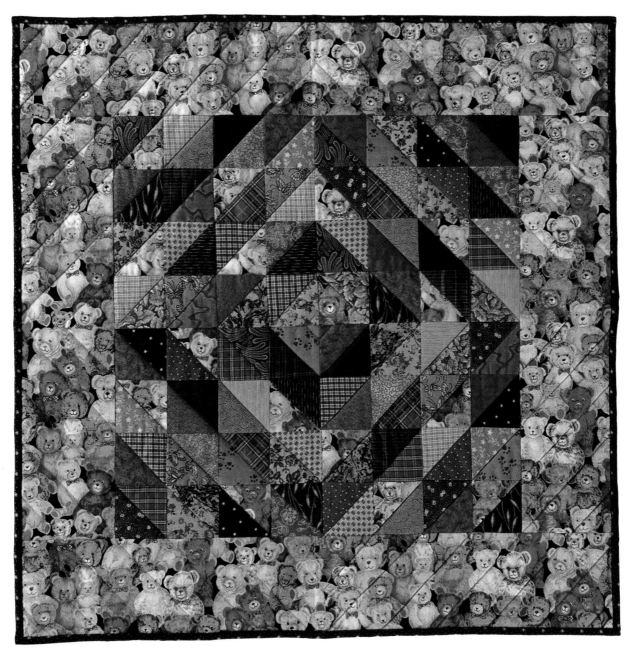

**"Teddy Bears' Picnic" by
Margaret Rolfe
35" x 35" (92 cm x 92 cm)
Block design 4**

Singing the Blues

BY JUDY HOOWORTH

Finished size: 43" (108 cm) square

Block design
Make 16

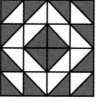

**Group of
four blocks**

YOU WILL NEED

Note: Fabric quantities are calculated for 44" (112 cm) wide fabric.

- ■ 3/4 yd (70 cm) of blue print fabric for the outer border
- ■ approximately 3/4 yd (70 cm) total of assorted blue print fabrics
- ■ approximately 3/4 yd (70 cm) total of assorted light purple print fabrics
- ■ 1/4 yd (25 cm) of purple solid fabric
- ■ small piece of turquoise solid fabric for the corner squares of the inner border
- ■ 48" x 48" (125 cm x 125 cm) piece of batting
- ■ 1 3/4 yds (160 cm) of print fabric for backing
- ■ 1/2 yd (50 cm) of purple print fabric for the binding
- ■ usual cutting, sewing and quilting supplies

CONSTRUCTION

1 Using the method of your choice (see pages 18–23) make sixty-eight half-square triangle units, 4" (10 cm) finished size, combining the assorted blue and light purple prints. If you are rotary cutting the triangles, cut 4 7/8" (12.5 cm) squares, cutting thirty-four squares each from the blue and light purple prints.

2 Assemble the half-square triangle units into sixteen blocks, following the block diagram.

3 Arrange the blocks into four rows of four blocks each, following the quilt diagram. Join the blocks into rows, then join the rows together to make the center of the quilt top.

For the borders:

1 From the fabric for the inner border, cut four 2" (5.5 cm) wide strips, cutting across the width of the fabric.

2 Always measuring the quilt top through its center to find the length required, trim the four strips to this length. Sew two strips to the sides of the quilt.

3 From the turquoise fabric, cut four 2" (5.5 cm) squares. Join the squares to each end of the two remaining border strips, then sew the strips to the top and bottom of the quilt.

4 From the fabric for the outer border, cut four 4 1/2" (11.5 cm) wide strips, cutting across the width of the fabric. Measure the quilt as before, then trim the four strips. Sew two strips to the sides of the quilt.

5 Join the remaining half-square triangle units to each end of the two remaining border strips, placing the blue triangle to the outside of the quilt. Sew the strips to the top and bottom of the quilt.

TO FINISH

1 Piece the backing fabric as required to make a 48" (125 cm) square.

2 Layer the backing, batting and quilt top. Pin-baste or thread-baste the layers together.

3 Quilt as desired.

4 From the binding fabric, cut five 3" (8 cm) wide strips. Join the strips together to achieve the length required. Bind the quilt.

"Singing the Blues" by
Judy Hooworth
43" x 43" (108 cm x 108 cm)
Block design 5

Redcurrent

BY JUDY HOOWORTH

YOU WILL NEED

Note: Fabric quantities are calculated for 44" (112 cm) wide fabric.

- 2 yds (1.7 m) of black-and-white print fabric for the fourth border (This quantity assumes a border without joins; if the fabric can be joined, only 1/2 yd (60 cm) is required.)
- 1 3/4 yds (1.6 m) of red print fabric for the third border
- approximately 1 1/2 yds (1.4 m) total of assorted red print fabrics
- approximately 1 1/2 yds (1.4 m) total of assorted black print fabrics
- 1/2 yd (40 cm) of purple print fabric for the first border
- 1/4 yd (25 cm) of black-and-white diagonal striped fabric for the second border
- 67" x 67" (169 cm x 169 cm) piece of batting
- 3 3/4 yds (3.5 m) of print fabric for the backing
- 3/4 yd (70 cm) of purple print fabric for the binding
- usual cutting, sewing and quilting supplies

Finished size: 63" (159 cm) square

Block design
Make 36

CONSTRUCTION

1 Using the method of your choice (see pages 18–23), make 144 half-square triangle units, 4" (10 cm) finished size, combining the assorted red and black prints. If you are rotary cutting the triangles, cut 4 7/8" (12.5 cm) squares, cutting seventy-two squares each from the red prints and black prints.

2 Assemble the half-square triangle units into thirty-six blocks, following the block diagram.

3 Join the blocks into six rows of six blocks each, following the quilt diagram. Join the rows to make the center of the quilt top.

For the borders:

1 From the purple print fabric for the first border, cut six 2" (5.5 cm) wide strips. Cut two strips in half and join these four halves to the remaining four uncut strips to achieve the required length.

2 From the black-and-white striped fabric for the second border, cut six 1" (3 cm) wide strips. Cut two strips in half and join these four halves to the remaining four uncut strips.

3 From the red print fabric for the third border, cut four 4 1/2" (11.5 cm) wide strips, cutting down the length of the fabric.

4 From the black-and-white print for the fourth border, cut four 2" (5.5 cm) wide strips, cutting down the length of the fabric. Alternatively, if the fabric can be joined, cut six 2" (5.5 cm) wide crosswise strips. Cut two strips in half and join these four halves to the remaining four uncut strips.

5 Pin-mark the center of each border strip, then join the strips together in their correct order, matching the pin-marked centers.

6 Following the method for making borders with mitered corners on page 26, add the borders to the quilt.

TO FINISH

1 Cut the backing fabric into two equal lengths and join the lengths, side by side. Trim to make a 67" (169 cm) square.

2 Layer the backing, batting and quilt top. Pin-baste or thread-baste the layers together.

3 Quilt as desired.

4 From the fabric for the binding, cut eight 3" (8 cm) wide strips. Join the strips to achieve the length required. Bind the quilt.

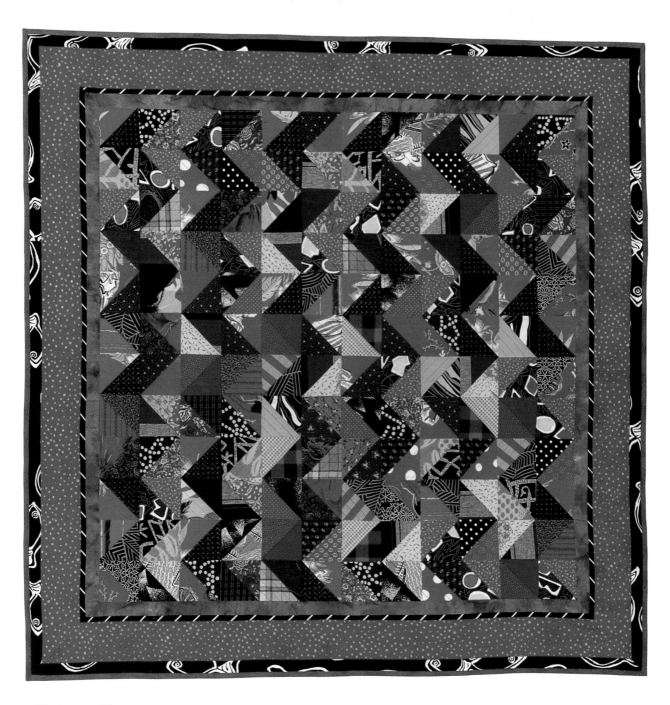

"Redcurrent" by
Judy Hooworth
63" x 63" (159 cm x 159 cm)
Block design 1

Find the Froggies

BY MARGARET ROLFE

YOU WILL NEED

Note: Fabric quantities are calculated for 44" (112 cm) wide fabric.

- 3/4 yd (50 cm) of bright multi-colored print fabric for the border
- approximately 1 yd (1 m) total of assorted pink and pink-related print fabrics (including yellow, red and orange)
- approximately 1 yd (1 m) total of assorted blue and blue-related print fabrics (including turquoise, green and purple)
- 40" x 54" (102 cm x 138 cm) piece of batting
- 1 1/2 yds (1.4 m) of fabric for the backing
- 1/2 yd (50 cm) of pink print fabric for the binding
- usual cutting, sewing and quilting supplies

Finished size: 36" x 50" (92 cm x 128 cm)

Block design
Make 24

CONSTRUCTION

1. Using the method of your choice (see pages 18–23), make ninety-six half-square triangle units, 3 1/2" (9 cm) finished size, combining the pink-related and the blue-related prints. If you are rotary cutting the triangles, cut 4 3/8" (11.5 cm) squares, cutting forty-eight squares each from the pink-related prints and the blue-related prints.

2. Assemble the half-square triangle units into twenty-four blocks, following the block diagram.

3. Arrange the blocks into six rows of four blocks each, following the quilt diagram. Join the blocks into rows, then join the rows to make the center of the quilt top.

For the border:

1. From the fabric for the border, cut four 4 1/2" (11.5 cm) wide strips.

2. Always measuring the quilt top through its center to find the lengths required, trim and sew two strips to the sides of the quilt, then trim and sew the remaining two strips to the top and bottom.

TO FINISH

1. Layer the backing, batting and quilt top. Pin-baste or thread-baste the layers together.

2. Quilt as desired.

3. From the fabric for the binding, cut five 2 1/2" (7 cm) wide strips. Join the strips to achieve the length required. Bind the quilt edges.

"Find the Froggies" by
Margaret Rolfe
36" x 50" (92 cm x 128 cm)
Block design 2

Kandy Kisses

BY JUDY HOOWORTH

YOU WILL NEED

Note: Fabric quantities are calculated for 44" (112 cm) wide fabric.

- 1³/4 yds (1.6 m) of **yellow-and-pink floral print fabric for the first border**
- approximately 1¹/4 yds (1.2 m) total of **assorted yellow print fabrics**
- approximately 1¹/4 yds (1.2 m) total of **assorted pink print fabrics**
- ³/4 yd (50 cm) of **yellow-and-pink striped fabric for the third border**
- ¹/4 yd (30 cm) of pink **solid fabric for the second border**
- 59" x 66" (151 cm x 169 cm) piece **of batting**
- 3¹/2 yds (3.4 m) of **fabric for the backing**
- ³/4 yd (60 cm) of **pink print fabric for the binding**
- usual cutting, sewing **and quilting supplies**

Finished size: 55" x 62" (141 cm x 159 cm)

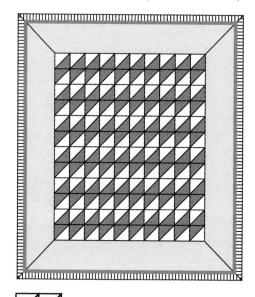

Block design
Make 30

CONSTRUCTION

1 Using the method of your choice (see pages 18–23), make 120 half-square triangle units, 3¹/2" (9 cm) finished size, combining the assorted yellow and pink print fabrics. If you are using rotary cutting methods, cut 4³/8" (11.5 cm) squares, cutting sixty squares from the yellow fabrics and sixty squares from the pink fabrics.

2 Assemble the half-square triangle units into thirty blocks, following the block design.

3 Arrange the blocks into six rows of five blocks each, as shown in the quilt diagram. Sew the blocks into rows, then join the rows to make the center of the quilt top.

For the borders:

1 From yellow-and-pink floral print fabric for the first border, and cutting down the length of the fabric, cut four 8" (21.5 cm) wide strips.

2 From the pink solid fabric for the second border, cut six 1¹/4" (3.5 cm) wide strips. Cut two of the strips in half and join these four pieces to the four uncut strips to achieve the required length.

3 From the yellow-and-pink striped fabric for the third border, and cutting across the width of the fabric, cut eight 2¹/4" (6 cm) wide strips. Join pairs of strips together, end to end, to make four long strips, matching the stripes at the joins.

4 Pin-mark the center of each border strip, then join the strips together in their correct order, matching the pin-marked centers.

5 Following the method for making borders with mitered corners (see page 26), add the border strips to the quilt.

TO FINISH

1 Cut the backing fabric into two equal lengths and join the lengths side by side. Trim to make a rectangle 59" x 66" (151 cm x 169 cm).

2 Layer the backing, batting and quilt top. Pin-baste or thread-baste the layers together.

3 Quilt as desired.

4 From the binding fabric, cut eight 3" (8 cm) wide strips. Join the strips to achieve the length required. Bind the quilt.

"Kandy Kisses" by
Judy Hooworth
55" x 62" (141 cm x 159 cm)
Block design 7

Gallery of Quilts

Opposite: "Twilight Roses" by Margaret Rolfe
56" x 56" (140 cm x 140 cm)
Block design 11
Above: "Cross of Amethyst" by Margaret Rolfe
38" x 38" (104 cm x 104 cm)
Block design 4

"Etoile" by
Margaret Rolfe
40" x 40" (112 cm x 112 cm)
Block design 13

"Yellow and Blue" by
Helen Gray
69" x 69" (175 cm x 175 cm)
Block design 2

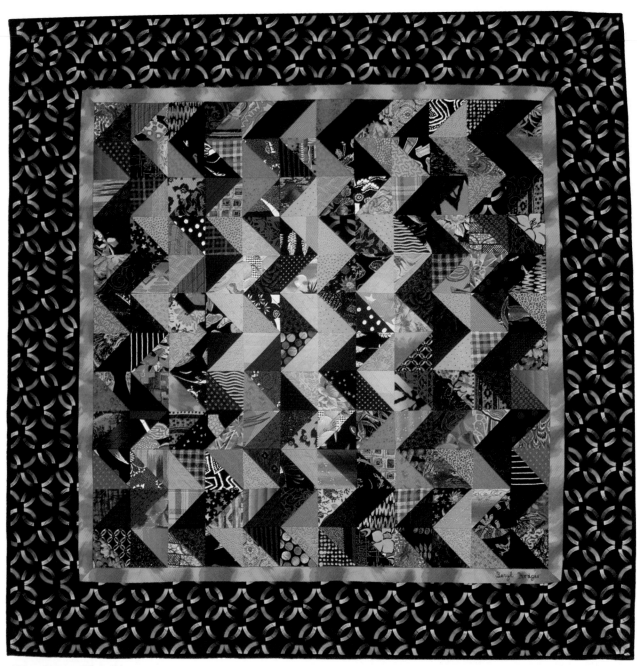

"Hot August Night" by
Beryl Hodges
65" x 65" (164 cm x 164 cm)
Block design 1

**"Sunset Over the Sea" by
Donna Ward
50" x 50" (126 cm x 126 cm)
Block design 5**

"Masquerade" by
Judy Hooworth
53" x 60" (136 cm x 154 cm)
Block design 4

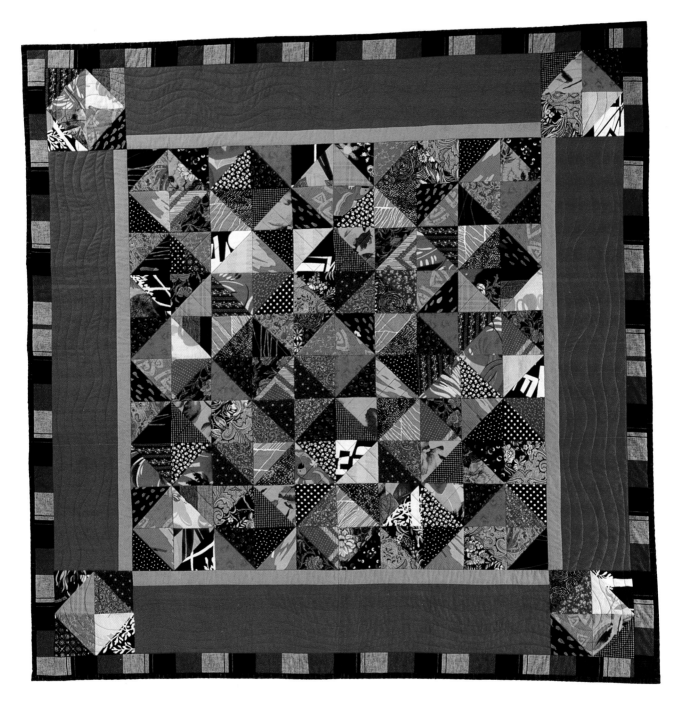

**"Earthworks" by
Judy Hooworth
61" x 61" (152 cm x 152 cm)
Block design 2**

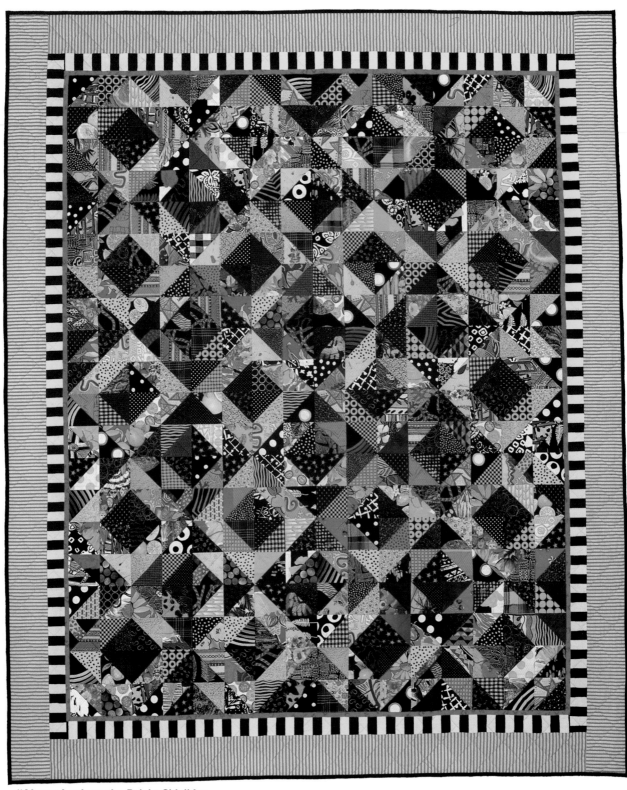

"Always Look on the Bright Side" by
Kerry Gavin
76" x 91" (192 cm x 232 cm)
Block design 5

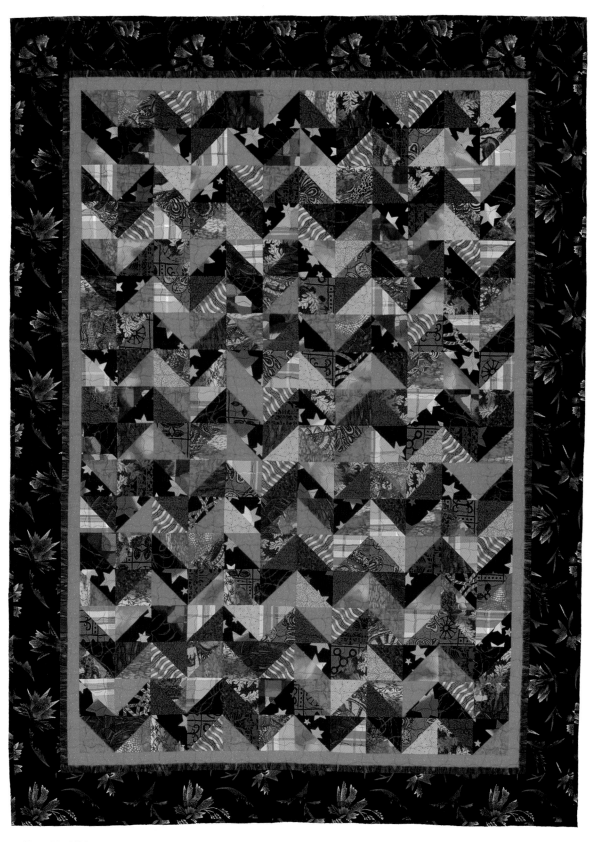

"Star Trek" by
Margaret Rolfe
62" x 86" (156 cm x 216 cm)
Block design 1

"Dit, Dot, Dash – Ginger Meggs' Mother Wears Spots" by
Kerry Gavin
75" x 82" (190 cm x 209 cm)
Block design 1

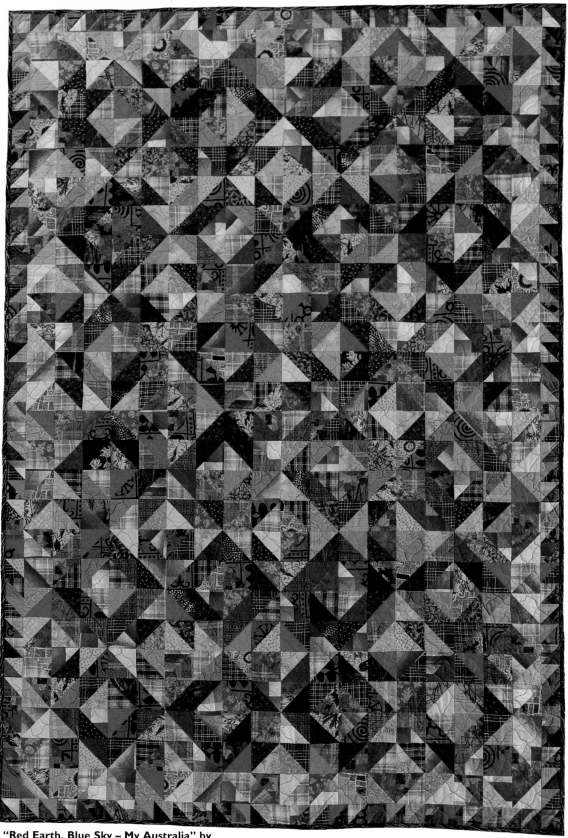

"Red Earth, Blue Sky – My Australia" by
Margaret Rolfe
58" x 82" (154 cm x 218 cm)
Block design 5

**"Singing in the Rain" by
Margaret Rolfe
56" x 56" (140 cm x 140 cm)
Block design 6**

"Printemps" by
Margaret Rolfe
84" x 92" (208 cm x 228 cm)
Block design 9

"Tiger Eyes" by
Margaret Rolfe
50" x 50" (128 cm x 128 cm)
Block design 5

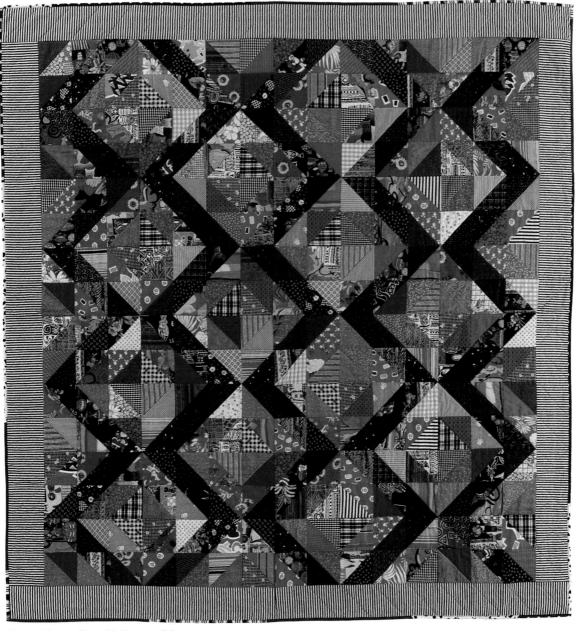

"Neon Lights Over Melbourne" by
Carol Richards
70" x 72" (178 cm x 184 cm)
Block of six half-square triangle units

Rotary cutting techniques

The size of a patchwork shape is usually referred to by its "finished size", which means its size as it will be seen in the quilt top. In other words, it is the size without the seam allowances added to it. Thus a 3" (8 cm) triangle is what you see in the quilt, but to make this shape, it must be cut out the finished size PLUS the seam allowances all around.

SEAM ALLOWANCE

Shapes cut out using a rotary cutter always include precisely cut seam allowances around them. The standard seam allowance for piecing using imperial measurements is $^1/4$", and for metric measurements it is 7.5 mm (0.75 cm). These particular measurements are chosen because they enable you to cut shapes in easily measured sizes.

It is very important that you sew the same seam allowance measurement that you have cut. Otherwise your shapes will not be accurate and will not join together exactly. The easiest way of maintaining an accurate seam allowance is to use the edge of the sewing machine presser foot as the guide. Consequently, the ideal situation is to have the distance between the needle and the edge of your presser foot exactly the same measurement as the seam allowance you are cutting. The best way to achieve this is to purchase a sewing machine foot that is specially made for an exact seam allowance, such as the $^1/4$" foot that is available for most machine models. Other alternatives are to move the position of the needle to make the exact distance, or to mark the bed of your machine with masking tape placed at the required distance.

USING THE ROTARY CUTTER

The rotary cutter is held in your dominant hand, right for right-handers and left for left-handers. The ruler is held down firmly with the other hand. The fabric is always cut along the side of the ruler that is next to the hand holding the rotary cutter (right side for right-handed people, left side for left-handed people). Here, the diagrams show the layout for right-handers, and we beg the forgiveness of left-handers who will need to do it the opposite way.

Safety is important. ALWAYS respect the sharpness of your rotary cutter, keeping fingers carefully away from the blade and closing the cutter every (we mean EVERY) time you put it down.

Note that up to four layers of fabric may be cut at any one time.

PREPARING THE FABRIC

Prepare for rotary cutting by first squaring up one side of your fabric. For this process you will need two rulers – a long one to make the cut and a shorter one to help you place the long ruler squarely on the fabric.

Place the shorter ruler on the fabric, making it square on the grain of the fabric and putting it near the fabric edge you wish to straighten. Place a long ruler directly alongside the smaller ruler and, being careful not to move the long ruler in any way, remove the smaller ruler and cut down the side of the long ruler. The edge should now be straight and on grain.

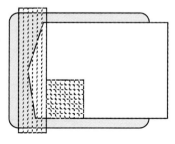
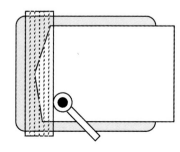

If the fabric is longer than your ruler, fold the fabric in half before cutting. More than one fold may be made for cutting long strips and borders. Place the fabric on the cutting mat with the fold immediately in front of you. When lining up the rulers to make the first cut, and for all subsequent cuts, make sure that the straight edge at the bottom of the ruler (or a line parallel to this edge) is exactly along the fold in the fabric. If you don't place the ruler exactly on the fold, when the fabric is opened out you will have cut a V-shaped edge rather than a straight one.

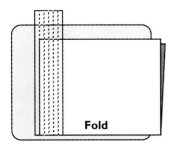

Fold

CUTTING SQUARES AND STRIPS

Place the ruler on top of the fabric, carefully lining up the prepared straight edge with the line on the ruler that is the distance you wish to cut. Cut down the side of the ruler.

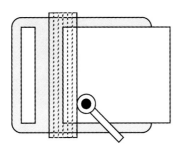

Trim the end of the strip so that it is exactly square.

Flip the strip around and, working from the squared-up end, cut squares by cutting the same measurement as the width of the strip.

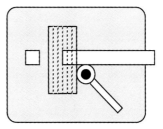

The measurement for cutting squares and rectangles that includes exact seam allowances is determined by adding $1/2$" (1.5 cm) to the size of the finished square desired.

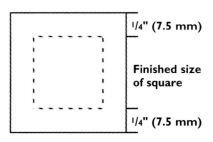

$1/4$" (7.5 mm)

Finished size of square

$1/4$" (7.5 mm)

Add $1/2$" (1.5 cm) to finished size of square or rectangle

CUTTING HALF-SQUARE TRIANGLES

Half-square triangles are cut from squares by cutting once across the diagonal. Each square makes two half-square triangles.

CUTTING QUARTER-SQUARE TRIANGLES

For quarter-square triangles, cut across both diagonals of the square, taking care that nothing is moved between the first and second diagonal cut.

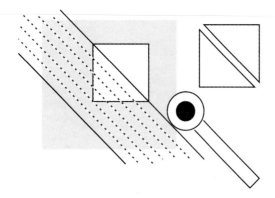

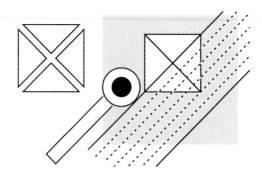

The measurement for cutting squares that will make two half-square triangles is determined by adding 7/8" (2.5 cm) to the finished size of a square that is made up of two half-square triangles.

The measurement for cutting squares that will make quarter-square triangles is determined by adding 1 1/4" (3.5 cm) to the finished size of a square that is made up of four quarter-square triangles.

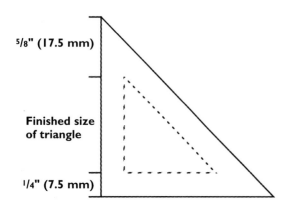

5/8" (17.5 mm)

Finished size of triangle

1/4" (7.5 mm)

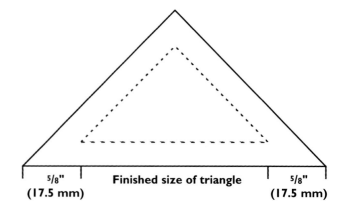

5/8" (17.5 mm)   **Finished size of triangle**   5/8" (17.5 mm)

Add 7/8" (2.5 cm) to finished size of triangle

Cut squares required size, then cut once diagonally

Add 1 1/4" (3.5 cm) to finished size of triangle

Cut squares required size, then cut across both diagonals

GRIDDED PAGE (FOR DESIGNING QUILTS)

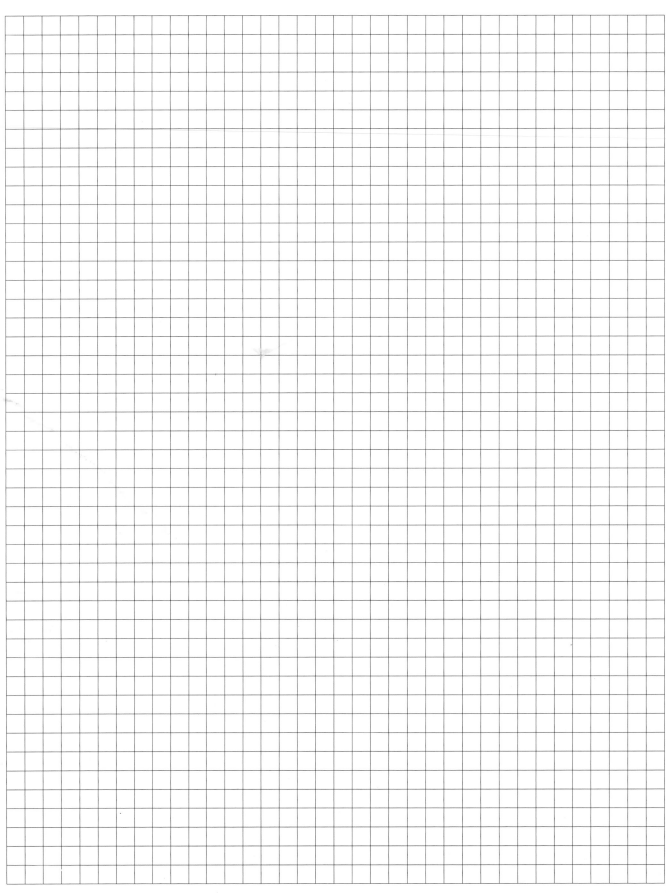